New Directions for
Community Colleges

Arthur M. Cohen
EDITOR-IN-CHIEF

Richard L. Wagoner
ASSOCIATE EDITOR

Gabriel Jones
MANAGING EDITOR

Presidents and Analysts Discuss Contemporary Challenges

John J. Prihoda
EDITOR

Number 156 • Winter 2011
Jossey-Bass
San Francisco

PRESIDENTS AND ANALYSTS DISCUSS CONTEMPORARY CHALLENGES
John J. Prihoda (ed.)
New Directions for Community Colleges, no. 156

Arthur M. Cohen, Editor-in-Chief
Richard L. Wagoner, Associate Editor
Gabriel Jones, Managing Editor

NEW DIRECTIONS FOR COMMUNITY COLLEGES (ISSN 0194-3081, electronic ISSN 1536-0733) is part of The Jossey-Bass Higher and Adult Education Series and is published quarterly by Wiley Subscription Services, Inc., A Wiley Company, at Jossey-Bass, One Montgomery, Ste. 1200, San Francisco, CA 94104. Periodicals Postage Paid at San Francisco, California, and at additional mailing offices. POSTMASTER: Send address changes to New Directions for Community Colleges, Jossey-Bass, One Montgomery, Ste. 1200, San Francisco, CA 94104.

SUBSCRIPTIONS cost $89.00 for individuals and $275.00 for institutions, agencies, and libraries in the United States. Prices subject to change.

EDITORIAL CORRESPONDENCE should be sent to the Editor-in-Chief, Arthur M. Cohen, at the Graduate School of Education and Information Studies, University of California, Box 951521, Los Angeles, CA 90095-1521. All manuscripts receive anonymous reviews by external referees.

New Directions for Community Colleges is indexed in CIJE: Current Index to Journals in Education (ERIC), Contents Pages in Education (T&F), Current Abstracts (EBSCO), Ed/Net (Simpson Communications), Education Index/Abstracts (H. W. Wilson), Educational Research Abstracts Online (T&F), ERIC Database (Education Resources Information Center), and Resources in Education (ERIC).

Microfilm copies of issues and articles are available in 16mm and 35mm, as well as microfiche in 105mm, through University Microfilms Inc., 300 North Zeeb Road, Ann Arbor, MI 48106-1346.

CONTENTS

EDITOR'S NOTES

Due to escalating retirements, we are witness to the largest exodus of experienced presidents and chancellors in community college history. Simultaneously, student populations are growing, demographics are shifting, and demands for student success are being redefined. All this is occurring while funding sources wither away.

The solutions to complex challenges facing new community college presidents are elusive. Charting new directions requires a thoughtful, insightful process that can include advice from respected sources. For insights into the future, presidents and chancellors (all recently retired) were asked to articulate significant issues, offer solutions, and comment on opportunities for our community colleges. In addition, eminent community college analysts were invited to review current college of education curricula to determine whether university programs meet contemporary needs. The result is *Presidents and Analysts Discuss Contemporary Challenges*, a uniquely authored volume in the annals of *New Directions for Community Colleges*. Originally intended to be a guide for new presidents, the depth of informative suggestions should also be helpful to a broad spectrum of those who champion the community college cause.

As readers will discover, even in retirement these authors remain deeply concerned about the welfare of this nation's noble educational invention, the American community college. I sincerely thank them for their dedication to this project.

JOHN J. PRIHODA, EdD, is retired president of Iowa Valley Community College District, IA, founding provost of Windward Community College, HI, and acting provost of Leeward Community College, HI.

NEW DIRECTIONS FOR COMMUNITY COLLEGES, no. 156, Winter 2011 © 2011 Wiley Periodicals, Inc.
Published online in Wiley Online Library (wileyonlinelibrary.com) • DOI: 10.1002/cc.461

1

*Never before have community colleges received so much
attention and recognition. From modest beginnings at the
start of the twentieth century, community colleges have
become the largest, most affordable, and most responsive
sector of American higher education. Policy makers,
media, and the public in general seem to have only now
discovered community colleges, which have been put
in a spotlight by President Barack Obama and leading
national foundations as important to the economic
prosperity of the United States. With increased attention
comes increased scrutiny, however. What will be expected
of community colleges, and how can they best respond,
especially given severe financial limitations? What are
their most pressing challenges, and what opportunities
are ahead for college leaders?*

Community Colleges in the Spotlight and Under the Microscope

George R. Boggs

Introduction

Community colleges owe their success to four enduring values: access, community responsiveness, creativity, and a focus on student learning. America's community colleges have provided access to higher education and an opportunity for a better life to the most diverse student body in history. The famous "open door" has welcomed students of all ages and ethnicities, students with disabilities, students with different learning objectives, and students with a wide difference in level of preparedness and prior educational experience. The colleges have responded to the needs of their local communities by developing partnerships with community businesses and agencies and by offering needed career programs, programs to retrain workers, and community service programs. In a higher education culture that does not often welcome change, community college leaders, faculty, and staff are among the most creative and innovative, experimenting with new methods to improve

New Directions for Community Colleges, no. 156, Winter 2011 © 2011 Wiley Periodicals, Inc.
Published online in Wiley Online Library (wileyonlinelibrary.com) • DOI: 10.1002/cc.462

the effectiveness of their teaching and to make services to students more convenient. Long known for quality teaching (Boyer, 1988), community colleges emerged in the 1990s as the leaders in focusing on the outcome of student learning as the core mission of higher education (Boggs, 1993b) and on the importance of closing achievement gaps and assisting more students to complete their educational goals (Boggs, 1993a).

These values, which have guided the philosophy of community colleges, will need to be protected in the future. Community colleges will soon be led by a new wave of administrators, faculty, and staff who will be replacing those who came into the system during the great growth period of the 1960s and 1970s (Shults, 2001). It is important that these professionals understand and value the unique role that community colleges play among the segments of higher education. College leaders will have to become more aggressive in seeking public and private funding in an environment that will be more competitive. Entrepreneurial initiatives and partnerships will be needed to stretch limited resources. More and better data will be needed to document the effectiveness of college programs in responding to increasing calls for accountability and to advocate effectively for these programs. The definition of "community" as "a climate to be created" (Boyer, 1988) will take on new meaning as distance education breaks down traditional geographic boundaries and as community colleges expand baccalaureate offerings. We will need to continue efforts to inform the public and policy makers of the important role that community colleges play in improving the life of individuals and in improving the economic viability of communities, our nation, and the world we live in.

Community colleges will need to expand capacities to accommodate increased numbers of students as greater percentages of Americans enter higher education. These institutions will be called on to take a more active role in K–12 reform and in preparing elementary and secondary school teachers. Community college faculty and public school teachers will need to be in more frequent contact to coordinate curriculum and to facilitate the transfer of students into college. Community colleges will expand their offerings of courses, especially in the use of technology, on high school campuses and will offer more professional development programs for school teachers.

Community colleges will have to become much more effective in closing student achievement gaps that exist for minority and low-income students, documenting student learning outcomes, and assisting more students to complete programs successfully. Barriers to degree completion and transfer to upper-division institutions will have to be overcome. College leaders should ensure that more of the students who qualify for financial aid actually receive it (College Board, 2010).

The increasing globalization of our economy and our society will require community colleges to continue to integrate international and cultural issues into the curriculum, to increase enrollments of international students, and to expand opportunities for students to study in other countries. Students will need preparation in the use of rapidly changing technology to interface with the world of the future. And technological advancements will continue to change how community colleges interact with students, providing services more conveniently and changing how faculty members teach and how students learn and communicate.

The Economy

The severe economic downturn of the late 2000s, sometimes referred to as "the Great Recession," was one of the major factors contributing to the national spotlight on community colleges. Factory closures and layoffs sent large numbers of displaced workers back to community colleges, where they hoped to pick up the skills needed to be reemployed. Major network television news stories and newspapers highlighted community colleges that were offering discounted tuition, midnight classes, and on-site counseling to the unemployed. By fall 2010, community college leaders also were reporting a significant increase in enrollments of younger students whose parents may have sent these recent high school graduates off to a university in better economic times.

Between 2008 and 2010, credit enrollment in community colleges surged by 17 percent (Mullin & Phillippe, 2009). In fact, half of all baccalaureate recipients (McPhee, 2006) and about one-third of science and engineering master's degree recipients have taken community college courses (Tsapogas, 2004). Forty percent of the nation's teachers complete some of their mathematics or science courses at these institutions (Shkodriani, 2004). Fifty percent of the nation's registered nurses (Institute of Medicine, 2010), over 80 percent of the first responders (American Association of Community Colleges, 2006), and most of the nation's technological workers are prepared in community colleges (American Association of Community Colleges, 2010). Forty-seven percent of first-generation college students, 53 percent of Hispanic, 45 percent of Black, 52 percent of Native American, and 45 percent of Asian/Pacific Islander students attend community colleges (American Association of Community Colleges, 2011d).

At the same time that community college student enrollment was surging, most states were responding to the economic downturn by cutting funding support. While federal stimulus funding, provided by the American Recovery and Reinvestment Act of 2009, provided temporary assistance to the states, the effects of the severe economic recession of the late 2000s will linger, creating significant problems for college leaders who are trying to respond to increased enrollment pressure with significantly less funding. Reports of students being turned away or not being able to enroll in the classes they need made national news in 2009 and 2010. Many economists predict that state economic problems will continue into 2011 (Katsinas & Friedel, 2010).

NEW DIRECTIONS FOR COMMUNITY COLLEGES • DOI: 10.1002/cc

The difficult economy, however, should provide some opportunities for changes that might be more difficult in better economic times. As Rahm Emanuel, President Obama's former chief of staff, famously said, "You never want a serious crisis to go to waste." Now may be the best time to focus on an institution's core mission, to discontinue programs that are least aligned to the mission, to eliminate waste and duplication, to improve efficiency, and to build a stronger private fundraising function. One likely positive outcome is that those younger students who are now at community colleges will tell others about the high-quality programs and care they received, leading to greater numbers of recent high school graduates starting at community colleges well into the future.

Funding problems, of course, did not start with the economic downturn. The trend toward state disinvestment in higher education has been ongoing even in good economic times (Policy Research Institute, 2010), and community colleges have been the higher education institutions most affected because of their reliance on taxpayer support. In a 2010 report from the American Association of Community Colleges, *Doing More with Less: The Inequitable Funding of Community Colleges*, Christopher Mullin (2010) points out that while community colleges serve 43 percent of all undergraduates (54 percent of all undergraduates in public higher education), they receive only 27 percent of total federal, state, and local higher education revenues. Community colleges are asked to educate the students who are most at risk with the least support, by far, of any other sector. If the United States is to meet the challenges of the future, policy makers must provide needed and more equitable support to colleges and universities and their students. Education at all levels must be seen as an important state and federal investment in our future, and policies must be put in place to ensure maximum return on that investment. Community college leaders must be prepared to become even more assertive in seeking necessary public support. The American Association of Community Colleges (2011e) has developed a public advocacy toolkit for college leaders that is available on its Web site.

College Completion

In the coming years, jobs requiring at least an associate degree are projected to grow twice as fast as those requiring no college experience (Carnevale, Smith, and Strohl, 2010). President Obama challenged the nation's community colleges to produce an additional 5 million program completers by 2020, an approximate 50 percent increase over current levels (Obama, 2009). In its report of the Springboard Project, the Business Roundtable (2009) echoed President Obama's challenge to increase education attainment levels in the United States in order to build a competitive workforce. The report recommended unlocking the value of community colleges, stating that these institutions have the potential to play a dominant role in strengthening local economies.

Despite the significant contributions of community colleges, student completion and transfer rates must improve dramatically if we are to meet President Obama's challenge. Too many students do not make it successfully through remedial programs into college-level courses, and too many do not complete their programs because of insufficient financial support or poor institutional or state policies and practices. The first significant effort to improve student completion in community colleges was set in motion by the Lumina Foundation for Education in 2004, with the launch of the national Achieving the Dream (ATD): Community Colleges Count initiative (Achieving the Dream, 2011). The goal of ATD is to help more community college students succeed, especially students of color, working adults, and students from low-income families. The ATD initiative emphasizes the use of data and the creation of a "culture of evidence" at the colleges to inform decision making and to measure progress against a specific set of student success metrics. Ultimately, Lumina's "Big Goal" is to increase the proportion of Americans with high-quality degrees and credentials to 60 percent by the year 2025 (Lumina Foundation for Education, 2010). The Organisation for Economic Co-Operation and Development (2009) rates the current educational attainment level for the United States at 40 percent.

Many community college students must overcome significant obstacles to complete their education: Many arrive unprepared for college-level work and must start in remedial courses; many are working at least part time while going to college; many have family responsibilities; some are single parents. They come to college wanting to succeed and to better their lives and to improve the well-being of their families. Through what we are learning in initiatives such as ATD, we can help more of them to complete their studies.

Begun with a cohort of 26 colleges, ATD has now expanded to 128 colleges in twenty-four states, including the District of Columbia. ATD efforts have focused on improving or expanding developmental education, gatekeeper courses, first-year experience, learning communities, academic and personal advising, student support services, and tutoring. A recent report indicated that the initiative is effectively increasing student persistence rates by as much as 13 percent (Jaschik, 2010). ATD colleges are working to strengthen linkages to K–12 and to engage the community. The initiative also is focused on changing state and federal policies that create barriers for students.

In 2009, the Bill & Melinda Gates Foundation announced a major postsecondary success initiative. The foundation is focused on ensuring that postsecondary education results in a degree or a certificate with genuine economic value. It has set an ambitious goal to double the number of young people who earn a postsecondary degree or certificate with value in the marketplace by the time they reach age twenty-six. The foundation notes that the types of jobs fueling our economy continue to change rapidly. Success in the workplace demands advanced skills in critical thinking and problem solving as well as the ability to shift readily from one task or project to another. Workers with strong language and math skills, technological capabilities, and a capacity to work well in teams are most likely to succeed. Carnevale, Smith, and Strohl (2010) project that, through 2018, nearly two-thirds (63 percent) of all new jobs will require more than a high school diploma; nearly half of those will require some college but less than a bachelor's degree. The Bureau of Labor Statistics projects that, through 2014, more than half of all new jobs will require more than a high school diploma (Hecker, 2005). Twenty-two of the fastest-growing career fields will require some postsecondary education (Bill & Melinda Gates Foundation, 2009). Speaking at the White House Summit on Community Colleges in October 2010, Melinda Gates told the audience that to meet the goals set by the foundation, the focus has to be on community colleges.

In April 2010, six national community college organizations representing trustees, administrators, faculty, and students signed a call to action to commit member institutions to match President Obama's 2020 goal (American Association of Community Colleges, 2011a). The organizations are currently seeking funding to develop cohesive and integrated strategies to move ahead, although challenges presented by the current economic climate that was already discussed could very well inhibit early progress. Nonetheless, these major associations are determined to move ahead with the "completion agenda."

College leaders and policy makers must also work to change state and institutional obstacles that block pathways for community college students to the baccalaureate degree because of poor transfer-of-credit policies. Organizations such as Complete College America (2011) and the National Governors Association (2011) appear ready to assist in improving these policies so that more students can complete baccalaureate and higher-level degrees. Phi Theta Kappa, the International Community College Honor Society, has launched CollegeFish.org to connect community college students to transfer institutions. Information is available on the Phi Theta Kappa Web site (Phi Theta Kappa, 2010).

In their 2009 book *Crossing The Finish Line*, Bowen, Chingos, and McPherson (2009) refer to research studies which find that students who start in community colleges are significantly less likely to attain a bachelor's degree than students who start in four-year universities. The authors concede that students who begin their studies at two-year colleges are very different from those who went directly to four-year schools, making it "foolish to simply compare the bachelor's degree attainment of these two groups" (p. 136). Community college students are more likely to be first-generation college students and less prepared for college; have a gap between high school graduation and college attendance; be place-bound, minority, female, less economically advantaged, working at least part-time; and not dependent on parents for financial support. In fact, many community college students have family obligations of their own, and many have to "stop out" of college to attend to family or work responsibilities.

Bowen, Chingos, and McPherson (2009) tried to adjust for some of the differences between the two- and four-year students by dividing them into "propensity" groups based on high school grades, Scholastic Achievement Test scores, gender, family income quartile, parental education, and educational aspirations. They used this method to define students with similar propensities to attain the baccalaureate and thus to compare students who started at community colleges with those who started at four-year institutions in a quasi-experiment. Their study, based on the North Carolina high school graduating class of 1999, showed an attainment disadvantage of starting in a community college of 26 to 36 percentage points for the ten propensity groups.

Similarly, Jones and Wellman, in a recent National Center for Higher Education Management Systems Delta Cost Project publication, called *Rethinking Conventional Wisdom about Higher Ed Finance* (2009), advise states against directing more students to community colleges to improve productivity. The authors say that, although costs per student are lower in community colleges, costs per degree are higher because they award so few degrees or credentials relative to student enrollment. The authors are quick to point out that they do not advise states to increase enrollments in public research universities. Perhaps an alternative would be to provide better funding to the least-well-funded institutions that are being asked to educate the most at-risk students.

In what might seem at first to be a contradiction to their earlier disparagement of community colleges, Bowen, Chingos, and McPherson (2009) also say that many four-year institutions could increase their own overall graduation rates while enrolling and graduating more low socioeconomic students by increasing their numbers of community college transfers. They say that transfer students do better in the university than if they had come directly from high school with the same credentials. In fact, they found that transfer students in the Maryland and North Carolina state systems graduated at substantially higher rates than did freshman enrollees.

These results should not really be surprising. Many studies show that community college transfers do at least as well as native university students after transferring, in terms of both grade point average and degree attainment. However, not enough community college students transfer. Some of this disparity is explained by how transfer data are collected. A 2001 study from the U.S. Department of Education National Center for Education Statistics looked at community college transfer rates using alternative definitions (Bradburn, Hurst, and Peng, 2001). One definition included only students who had declared an academic major and were taking courses that led toward a baccalaureate. Using this definition, 52 percent of the students successfully transferred. Using a broader definition of those students who simply say they want to earn a bachelor's degree or higher resulted in a finding of only 36 percent who transferred.

Today's college students are more mobile than ever, frequently taking courses at more than one institution on their way to a baccalaureate. Using data from the National Center for Education Statistics Baccalaureate and Beyond Longitudinal Study, an American Association of Community Colleges (AACC) Research Report, *En Route to the Baccalaureate: Community College Student Outcomes* (McPhee, 2006), found that half of the 1999–2000 baccalaureate recipients in the United States attended a community college prior to obtaining the baccalaureate. However, students often face policy barriers that make transfer difficult. Significant differences in the ease of transfer exist from one state to another. Students frequently lose credit for courses they have taken, causing frustration and delay, while adding to costs for both students and taxpayers. The loss of credit also negatively affects the degree attainment rate. A study by Doyle (2006) showed that 82 percent of the students who had all of their courses accepted by the four-year institution completed a baccalaureate within six years; the rate was reduced to 42 percent when only some credits were accepted. These barriers exist despite the fact that community colleges and transfer universities are accredited by the same agencies.

All too often, universities treat community college transfers as buffers in maintaining desired enrollment numbers. When enrollments are needed, universities allow more transfer students to be admitted. When enrollment pressure is too high or funding is cut, universities often make it more difficult or impossible for students to transfer in. Bowing to political pressure from parents, universities often give preference to entering freshmen over transfer students who do not have other options. Bowen, Chingos, and McPherson (2009) report that 1,719 transfer applicants were recently rejected by the average public university in California; 1,092 in Florida; and an average of 405 by universities in each of the other forty-eight states and the District of Columbia.

Community colleges are designed to be convenient for students. Campuses are located within commuting distance of over 90 percent of the U.S. population, and community colleges are leaders in distance education. Recently, Bunker Hill Community College in Boston was featured for offering "midnight classes." It is common for community colleges to offer early-morning and late-night classes, classes in community centers, short-term classes, long-term classes, and intersession classes. The colleges cater to students who are place-bound, disabled, working, or raising a family. It is not feasible for many of these students to leave their communities to transfer to a university. Several community colleges have established university centers on their campuses or have even begun to offer their own bachelor's degrees in selected fields so that students can continue their education.

President Obama has made increased degree completion an important goal for our country. He has also recognized that community colleges, which now enroll nearly half of all undergraduate credit students (American Association of Community Colleges, 2011d), are essential if the goal is to be achieved. It is long past time for community college and university educators and state and federal policy makers to work toward removing the barriers that require students to clear unnecessary hurdles that are keeping too many of them from degree achievement.

Accountability and Advocacy

For some time, pressure has been building for institutions of higher education both to improve outcomes for students and to provide greater accountability to the public and other stakeholders. This renewed accountability movement was given sharper focus by the discussions and recommendations of Education Secretary Margaret Spellings's Commission on the Future of Higher Education (2006), which issued its final report in 2006. The commission, reflecting the views of a growing number of policy makers, painted a critical picture of American higher education as being arrogant, unconcerned about escalating costs, and unwilling to change. While public regard for community colleges has improved in recent years, the institutions are often swept into the same federal and state regulations that are designed for universities and for-profit training institutions.

The university sectors responded to the Spellings Commission by developing a Voluntary System of Accountability (AASCU/APLU, 2011) for public institutions and the University and College Accountability Network (U-CAN) (National Association of Independent Colleges and Universities, 2011) for independent institutions. The two systems have continued to develop and, in particular, provide valuable consumer information for students and families. However, neither VSA nor U-CAN provide a very suitable model for a community college framework for accountability.

Lack of commonly accepted performance measures for community colleges has often led to a misunderstanding of the institutions and an underestimation of their effectiveness and their contributions. Recognizing that community colleges need a process through which they communicate data that paint the most accurate portrait of the sector and its unique role in American higher education, AACC, the Association of Community College Trustees, and the College Board launched a Voluntary Framework of Accountability (VFA) initiative in 2009 (American Association of Community Colleges, 2011f). The initiative, funded by the Lumina Foundation for Education and the Bill & Melinda Gates Foundation, is currently at the pilot-testing stage.

Certainly, the multiple missions of community colleges complicate how institutional performance is measured. Students enter a community college for diverse reasons. Some enroll to prepare for a career; others attend for a single course to upgrade a specific job skill, perhaps to earn a promotion; others seek a baccalaureate by completing their lower-division courses at a community college and transfer to a four-year college or university. Still others enter community colleges for personal enrichment alone. The varied needs and individual goals of community college students, which represent appropriate and vital aspects of the community college mission, are difficult to measure in meaningful ways.

Current methodologies measuring higher education productivity do not capture well the work of community colleges or the students who attend them. The federal Integrated Postsecondary Education Data System (IPEDS), for example, is focused on measuring the amount of time it takes for a student to complete a degree or certificate. While this represents an important dimension of productivity, it describes little of what is actually going on at community colleges. There are at least three reasons for this:

1. Only first-time, full-time students are included in the IPEDS calculation for time to degree, while 62 percent of community college students are enrolled part-time.
2. "Success" on current assessments is defined as the completion of a degree or certificate, yet the educational goals of community college students vary widely, often in ways both richer and more idiosyncratic than traditional academic measures of completion.
3. Even in those instances in which two- and four-year institutional goals overlap, community colleges do not receive credit for the work they do. A case in point is transfer. While community colleges prepare thousands of students for transfer to four-year institutions and the baccalaureate, the students who transfer from their institutions before attaining an associate degree are classified as drop-outs. Transfer data are not usually systematically reported back to the community colleges, and community colleges are regularly and often unjustly criticized for having low transfer rates.

The VFA initiative is now in phase II, which will result in the final measurement definitions, a plan for collection and delivery of the metrics, and a plan to market the final service to all community colleges. The project will be accomplished through the work of the VFA steering committee and working groups and from additional community college professionals nationally. The VFA steering committee, comprised of community college presidents and nationally recognized assessment experts, is providing direction to the working groups and project staff. Four working groups are developing and refining the VFA metrics. The first working group focuses on student persistence and completion measures including such traditional metrics as retention, transfer, and completion. Other metrics will be explored to identify ways to measure student progress toward completion such as reaching credit milestones.

The second working group is identifying appropriate learning outcomes for community college students and discussing a process and method for properly assessing and reporting learning outcomes. The third working group is examining metrics related to workforce, economic, and community development. These metrics are a critical part of what community colleges do and must be considered in any framework that attempts to assess the efficacy of community colleges. The fourth working group is developing a plan to gain near-universal community college buy-in for the VFA. This group will review feedback on college reactions (acceptance and resistance) to participating in the VFA and will develop messages that can be used to promote its widespread use.

The current lack of acceptable accountability measures for community colleges presents a challenge to community college leaders who do not have the necessary information to describe to policy makers and the public just how effective their institutions are. Moreover, accurate baseline information is essential for college leaders, faculty, and staff to set goals for improvement in outcomes. The VFA and its refinements should provide an answer to the need for more accurate and relevant information.

Leadership Development

The current and projected turnover of community college leadership presents significant challenges, as we must prepare leaders who understand and value the community college mission and who have the skills needed to be effective leaders in a challenging environment. However, the turnover also provides an opportunity to bring new energy and greater diversity into the leadership of the community college movement.

While the founding leaders of the community college movement were the pioneers and the builders, today's leaders operate in a more complex world. Resources are constrained, accountability requirements are increasing, labor relations are becoming more contentious, and society is more litigious than ever before. Learning opportunities and services are now expected to be offered twenty-four hours a day, seven days a week. Distance learning technologies are erasing geographical boundaries, and competition for students will increase.

College leaders are expected to respond ever more quickly to meet emerging community and national needs. Community colleges are being asked to respond to the shortage of healthcare workers and teachers, to develop new programs for emerging technologies, and to prepare students to live in an increasingly global society and economy—all with declining financial resources.

Respondents to periodic AACC surveys reveal that presidents do not feel prepared for several aspects of community college leadership. They indicate surprise by the overwhelming demands of the job. Community college leadership can be all-consuming, and the more responsibility one has, the more time it takes to do a good job. Community college leaders are called on to perform official duties in the evenings, on weekends, and even while on vacation. Because of the time commitment, presidents often have difficulty in balancing their professional, private, and spiritual lives.

NEW DIRECTIONS FOR COMMUNITY COLLEGES • DOI: 10.1002/cc

Presidents often report being lonely at the top. Because faculty members and mid-level administrators always have peers at the institution who are doing almost the same job, there are others from whom to seek advice and with whom to commiserate. But there is only one president. At the same time that presidents report being alone, they are also very visible, recognized, and set apart by the uniqueness of their position. The AACC Presidents Academy responds to the need to provide professional development for community college chief executive officers (CEOs) and to provide them with a network of support (Boggs, 2002).

Relationship building is an important part of a leader's responsibilities. In order to advance the mission of the college, it is essential to have the active support of all college constituencies. External relationships can give the college support in the form of resources, facilities, and goodwill. However, many leaders report being unprepared to deal with both internal and external relationships.

Fundraising and financial management are two skills for which presidents report a lack of preparation. Since community colleges are the most insufficiently financed institutions of American higher education, it is important for the presidents to understand increasingly complex fiscal principles. College leaders do not have the luxury of making financial mistakes. Community college leaders are not as experienced as are their colleagues in other sectors of higher education in raising private funds. With projections of declining public revenues for colleges, these skills will be more important.

Presidents often report being unprepared for their work with governing boards. In fact, stories of problems between presidents and boards abound, and too many of them make national news. Sometimes presidents look for ways to survive their boards rather than seeing themselves and their boards as teams that provide direction to a complex enterprise (Boggs, 2006).

All too often, community college faculty and leaders are subjected to incivility within their campus communities. Leaders, in particular, are sometimes subjected to excessive criticism and, occasionally, harassment. It has somehow become acceptable to attack college leaders, whether they are administrators, faculty members, staff, or students. Perhaps this has been caused by governance struggles, difficult labor negotiations, or autocratic behavior. Whatever the cause, leaders must learn how to improve the climate on community college campuses (Boggs, 2005).

While there has been some progress in bringing greater gender diversity to community college leadership, there has been much less progress with ethnic diversity (see Figure 1.1). In maintaining its membership database, AACC (2011c) regularly gathers demographic data on community college CEOs and participants in its Future Leaders Institutes (FLIs). To promote diversity among the future leaders of community colleges, AACC also works actively to encourage member colleges to value diversity in

Figure 1.1. Demographic Breakdown of Community College CEOs

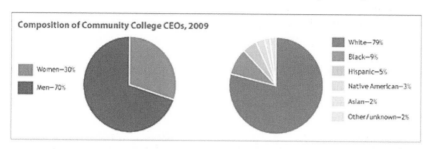

Composition of Community College CEOs, 2009

Women—30%
Men—70%

White—79%
Black—9%
Hispanic—5%
Native American—3%
Asian—2%
Other/unknown—2%

Composition of Future Leader Institute Participants, 2003–2009

Gender and Race/Ethnicity	FLI		FLI Advanced		
	Number	Percent	Number	Percent	Total
Gender					
Men	221	45%	73	50%	294
Women	267	55%	72	50%	339
Race/Ethnicity					
White	352	72%	110	76%	
Black	90	18%	25	17%	115
Hispanic	7	1%	2	1%	9
Asian	31	6%	5	3%	36
Other	8	2%	3	2%	11
TOTAL	488		145		633

Note: Data are based on FLI and FLI Advanced alumni records from 2008–2009 classes. Alumni who completed both classes (25) are counted in each class.

nominating candidates for attendance at its premier professional development program, the FLI.

Leadership and faculty development programs and institutes must do a better job of preparing a diverse group of people to meet the challenges of leadership. What we know about both leadership competencies and the problems that current leaders are facing should be a guide for developing the curriculum needed for institutes, mentorships, and doctoral programs. Current community college leaders and trustees should understand that one of their most important responsibilities is to mentor and prepare the next generation of leaders. Future leaders will be selected because of their demonstrated knowledge and skills. They will need opportunities to learn, develop, and practice these skills through participation in leadership institutes and seminars, internships, and mentorships. Leadership programs should be structured to provide these opportunities for skill development.

In April 2005, after broad participation from the field and with support from the W. K. Kellogg Foundation, the AACC board of directors approved its competencies for community college leadership (2011b). The competencies are available from the AACC Web site and have been used by many community college leadership development programs and institutes. A description of the six competencies is given next.

Organizational Strategy. An effective community college leader strategically improves the quality of the institution, protects the long-term health of the organization, promotes the success of all students, and sustains the community college mission, based on knowledge of the organization, its environment, and future trends.

Illustrations:

- Assess, develop, implement, and evaluate strategies regularly to monitor and improve the quality of education and the long-term health of the organization.
- Use data-driven evidence and proven practices from internal and external stakeholders to solve problems, make decisions, and plan strategically.
- Use a systems perspective to assess and respond to the culture of the organization; to changing demographics; and to the economic, political, and public health needs of students and the community.
- Develop a positive environment that supports innovation, teamwork, and successful outcomes.
- Maintain and grow college personnel and fiscal resources and assets.
- Align organizational mission, structures, and resources with the college master plan.

Resource Management. An effective community college leader equitably and ethically sustains people, processes, and information as well as physical and financial assets to fulfill the mission, vision, and goals of the community college.

Illustrations:

- Ensure accountability in reporting.
- Support operational decisions by managing information resources and ensuring the integrity and integration of reporting systems and databases.
- Develop and manage resource assessment, planning, budgeting, acquisition, and allocation processes consistent with the college master plan and local, state, and national policies.
- Take an entrepreneurial stance in seeking ethical alternative funding sources.
- Implement financial strategies to support programs, services, staff, and facilities.
- Implement a human resources system that includes recruitment, hiring, reward, and performance management systems and that fosters the professional development and advancement of all staff.
- Employ organizational, time management, planning, and delegation skills.

• Manage conflict and change in ways that contribute to the long-term viability of the organization.

Communication. An effective community college leader uses clear listening, speaking, and writing skills to engage in honest, open dialogue at all levels of the college and its surrounding community, to promote the success of all students, and to sustain the community college mission.

Illustrations:
• Articulate and champion shared mission, vision, and values to internal and external audiences, appropriately matching message to audience.
• Disseminate and support policies and strategies.
• Create and maintain open communications regarding resources, priorities, and expectations.
• Convey ideas and information succinctly, frequently, and inclusively through media and verbal and nonverbal means to the board and other constituencies and stakeholders.
• Listen actively to understand, comprehend, analyze, engage, and act.
• Project confidence and respond responsibly and tactfully.

Collaboration. An effective community college leader develops and maintains responsive, cooperative, mutually beneficial, and ethical internal and external relationships that nurture diversity, promote the success of all students, and sustain the community college mission.

Illustrations:
• Embrace and employ the diversity of individuals, cultures, values, ideas, and communication styles.
• Demonstrate cultural competence relative to a global society.
• Catalyze involvement and commitment of students, faculty, staff, and community members to work for the common good.
• Build and leverage networks and partnerships to advance the mission, vision, and goals of the community college.
• Work effectively and diplomatically with unique constituent groups such as legislators, board members, business leaders, accreditation organizations, and others.
• Manage conflict and change by building and maintaining productive relationships.
• Develop, enhance, and sustain teamwork and cooperation.
• Facilitate shared problem solving and decision making.

Community College Advocacy. An effective community college leader understands, commits to, and advocates for the mission, vision, and goals of the community college.

Illustrations:

- Value and promote diversity, inclusion, equity, and academic excellence.
- Demonstrate a passion for and commitment to the mission of community colleges and student success through the scholarship of teaching and learning.
- Promote equity, open access, teaching, learning, and innovation as primary goals for the college, seeking to understand how these change over time and facilitating discussion with all stakeholders.
- Advocate the community college mission to all constituents and empower them to do the same.
- Advance lifelong learning and support a learner-centered and learning-centered environment.
- Represent the community college in the local community, in the broader educational community, at various levels of government, and as a model of higher education that can be replicated in international settings.

Professionalism.   An effective community college leader works ethically to set high standards for self and others, continuously improve self and surroundings, demonstrate accountability to and for the institution, and ensure the long-term viability of the college and community.

Illustrations:

- Demonstrate transformational leadership through authenticity, creativity, and vision.
- Understand and endorse the history, philosophy, and culture of the community college.
- Self-assess performance regularly using feedback, reflection, goal-setting, and evaluation.
- Support lifelong learning for self and others.
- Manage stress through self-care, balance, adaptability, flexibility, and humor.
- Demonstrate the courage to take risks, make difficult decisions, and accept responsibility.
- Understand the impact of perceptions, worldviews, and emotions on self and others.
- Promote and maintain high standards for personal and organizational integrity, honesty, and respect for people.
- Use influence and power wisely in facilitating the teaching-learning process and the exchange of knowledge.
- Weigh short-term and long-term goals in decision making.
- Contribute to the profession through professional development programs, professional organizational leadership, and research/publication.

NEW DIRECTIONS FOR COMMUNITY COLLEGES • DOI: 10.1002/cc

Future community college leaders must be models of integrity, honesty, and high ethical standards. They must be open to new ideas, and their judgments must be fair, dispassionate, and equitable. They must confront issues and people without prejudice. In particular, they must ensure that students are respected as individual learners and protected from disparagement, embarrassment, or capricious behavior. They must realize that retaining their popularity is not as important as doing what is right. To be successful in today's environment and that of the future, leaders must find ways to involve people in their decisions. They must be catalysts for finding ways to make things happen for the college and its people. They should encourage and support innovation and discovery. Today's leaders must play a significant role in shaping the community college leadership of the future.

Conclusion

In the complex environment in which community colleges operate today and in which they will operate in the future, the challenges seem almost overwhelming. Challenges include calls to:

- Close achievement gaps for students
- Increase course and program completion rates
- Provide evidence of student learning
- Prepare students to succeed in a global economy and society
- Increase the number of students who transfer successfully to universities
- Prepare students for employment in emerging economies
- Reposition the colleges to thrive with declining public resources
- Advocate more effectively for public resources by demonstrating how important community colleges are to economic vitality and to the well-being of communities
- Become more entrepreneurial in developing partnerships and raising private resources, to become more accountable for institutional outcomes
- Mentor and support new faculty and aspiring leaders
- Bring greater diversity to community college leadership
- Develop positive and productive relationships with boards of trustees and with other policy makers.

However, each of these challenges presents opportunities for leaders to strengthen their colleges and thereby the communities they serve. America's community colleges have become the envy of other nations throughout the world. Their continued success will depend on those who lead and govern these unique institutions.

References

Achieving the Dream. *Strategies at Achieving the Dream Colleges.* 2011. http://www
.achievingthedream.org/campusstrategies/strategiesatachievingthedreamcolleges
/default.tp.
American Association of Community Colleges. *First Responders: Community Colleges on
the Front Line of Security.* Washington, D.C.: Author, 2006. http://www.aacc.nche.edu
/Publications/Reports/Documents/firstresponders.pdf.
American Association of Community Colleges. *Community Colleges Serving Communities
Strengthening the Nation.* Washington, D.C.: Community College Press, American
Association of Community Colleges, 2010.
American Association of Community Colleges. *College Completion Challenge: A Call to
Action.* Washington, D.C.: Author, 2011a. http://www.aacc.nche.edu/About/Pages
/calltoaction.aspx.
American Association of Community Colleges. *Competencies for Community College
Leadership.* Washington, D.C.: Author, 2011b.
American Association of Community Colleges. *Diversity, Inclusion, and Equity.*
Washington, D.C.: Author, 2011c.
American Association of Community Colleges. *Fast Facts.* Washington, D.C.: Author,
2011d. http://www.aacc.nche.edu/AboutCC/Pages/fastfacts.aspx.
American Association of Community Colleges. *Public Advocacy Toolkit.* Washington,
D.C.: Author, 2011e. http://www.aacc.nche.edu/Advocacy/toolkit/Pages/default
.aspx.
American Association of Community Colleges. *Voluntary Framework of Accountability.*
Washington, D.C.: Author, 2011f.
American Association of State Colleges and Universities/Association of Public and Land
Grant Universities. *Voluntary System of Accountability.* Washington, D.C.: Author,
2011. http://www.voluntarysystem.org/index.cfm.
Bill & Melinda Gates Foundation. *Postsecondary Success.* Redmond, Wash.: Author,
2009. http://www.gatesfoundation.org/postsecondaryeducation.
Boggs, G. "Leaders Must Make Diversity Issues a College Priority." *Community College
Journal,* 1993a, 64(3), 4–5.
Boggs, G. "Reinventing Community Colleges." *Community College Journal,* 1993b,
64(3), 4–5.
Boggs, G. *Civility on Campus.* In P. Elsner and G. Boggs (eds.), *Encouraging Civility as a
Community College Leader.* Washington, D.C.: Community College Press, American
Association of Community Colleges, 2005, 1–12.
Boggs, G. *Handbook on CEO-Board Relations and Responsibilities.* Washington, D.C.:
Community College Press, 2006.
Boggs, G., with Kent, E. L. "Presidents Academy: An Evolution of Leadership Develop-
ment." In G. E. Watts (ed.), *Enhancing Community Colleges Through Professional
Development.* New Directions in Community Colleges, no. 120 San Francisco: Jossey-
Bass, 2002, 51–57.
Bowen, W., Chingos, M., and McPherson, M. *Crossing the Finish Line: Completing Col-
lege at America's Public Universities.* Princeton, N.J.: Princeton University Press, 2009.
Boyer, E. *Building Communities: A Vision for a New Century.* Report of the Commission
on the Future of Community Colleges. Washington, D.C.: American Association of
Community Colleges, 1988.
Bradburn, E. M., Hurst, D. G., and Peng, S. *Community College Transfer Rates to 4-year
Institutions Using Alternative Definitions of Transfer.* NCES 2001–197. Washington,
D.C.: Office of Educational Research and Improvement, National Center for Educa-
tion Statistics, June 2001.
Business Roundtable. *Getting Ahead—Staying Ahead. Helping America's Workforce Suc-
ceed in the 21st Century.* Washington, D.C.: Author, 2009. http://businessroundtable

.org/studies-and-reports/the-springboard-project-releases-final-recommendations-to -strengthen-a/

Carnevale, A., Smith, N., & Strohl, J. *Help Wanted: Projections of Jobs and Education Requirements Through 2018.* Washington, D.C.: Georgetown University, Center on Education and the Workforce, 2010.

College Board. *The Financial Aid Challenge: Successful Practices That Address the Under- utilization of Financial Aid in Community Colleges.* New York, N.Y.: College Board, 2010.

Complete College America. "The Path Forward." Washington, D.C., 2011. http://www .completecollege.org/path_forward/.

Doyle, W. R. "Community College Transfers and College Graduation: Whose Choices Matter Most?" *Change,* May/June 2006, 56–58.

Hecker, D. E. "Occupational Employment Projections to 2014." *Monthly Labor Review,* November 2005, 80.

Institute of Medicine. *The Future of Nursing: Leading Change, Advancing Health.* Washington, D.C.: Author, 2010. http://www.iom.edu/Reports/2010/The-Future -of-Nursing-Leading-Change-Advancing-Health.aspx

Jaschik, S. "Moving the Needle." *Inside Higher Ed,* 2010, June 1. http://www .insidehighered.com/news/2010/06/01/nisod.

Jones, D., and Wellman, J. *Rethinking Conventional Wisdom about Higher Ed Finance.* Boulder, Colo.: National Center for Higher Education Management Systems, 2009. http://www.deltacostproject.org/resources/pdf/advisory_10_Myths.pdf.

Katsinas, S., and Friedel, J. *Uncertain Recovery: Access and Funding Issues in Public Higher Education.* Tuscaloosa: University of Alabama Press, 2010.

Lumina Foundation for Education. "Goal 2025." 2010. http://www.luminafoundation .org/goal_2025/.

McPhee, S. *En Route to the Baccalaureate: Community College Student Outcomes.* (AACC Research Brief AACC-RB-06-1.) Washington, D.C.: American Association of Community Colleges, 2006. http://www.aacc.nche.edu/Publications/Briefs/Pages/rb09182006.aspx.

Mullin, C. *Doing More With Less: The Inequitable Funding of Community Colleges.* (AACC Policy Brief 2010–03PBL.) Washington, D.C.: American Association of Community Colleges, 2010. http://www.aacc.nche.edu/Publications/Briefs/Pages/rb09082010 .aspx.

Mullin, C., and Phillippe, K. *Community College Enrollment Surge: An Analysis of Esti- mated Fall 2009 Headcount Enrollments at Community Colleges.* (Policy Brief 2009–01 PBL.) Washington, D.C.: American Association of Community Colleges, 2009. http:// www.aacc.nche.edu/Publications/Briefs/Pages/rb12172009.aspx.

National Association of Independent Colleges and Universities. *University and College Accountability Network.* Washington, D.C.: Author, 2011. http://www.ucan-network .org/.

National Governors Association. *Complete to Compete.* Washington, D.C.: Author, 2011. http://www.subnet.nga.org/ci/1011/2011.

Obama, B. "Remarks by the President on the American Graduation Initiative." Washington, D.C.: The White House, Office of the Press Secretary, July 14, 2009. http://www.whitehouse.gov/the_press_office/Remarks-by-the-President-on-the -American-Graduation-Initiative-in-Warren-MI/.

Organisation for Economic Co-Operation and Development. "Education at a Glance 2009: OECD Indicators." 2009. www.oecd.org/edu/eag2009.

Phi Theta Kappa. *CollegeFish.org.* Jackson, Miss.: Author, 2010. http://www .collegefish.org/help/ptk-students-cf-guide.pdf.

Policy Research Institute. "How to Fix a Broken System: Funding Public Higher Educa- tion and Making It More Productive: Setting a Pathway to Greater Productivity Within New Funding Realities." Princeton, N.J.: New Jersey Association of State Col- leges and Universities, 2010. http://www.njascu.org/PolicyBriefApril2010.pdf.

Shkodriani, G. *Seamless Pipeline from Two-Year to Four-Year Institutions for Teacher Train-ing*. Denver, Colo.: Education Commission of the States, 2004. http://www.ecs.org /html/Document.asp?chouseid = 4957.

Shults, C. *The Critical Impact of Impending Retirements on Community College Leadership*. (Research Brief AACC-RB-01–5.) Washington, D.C.: American Association of Community Colleges, 2001.

Spellings, M. *Report of the Commission on the Future of Higher Education*. Washington, D.C.: U.S. Department of Education, 2006. http://www2.ed.gov/about/bdscomm/list /hiedfuture/reports/final-report.pdf.

Tsapogas, J. *The Role of Community Colleges in the Education of Recent Science and Engineering Graduates*. Arlington, Va.: National Science Foundation, 2004. http:// www.nsf.gov/statistics/infbrief/nsf04315/.

GEORGE R. BOGGS is the president and CEO emeritus of the American Association of Community Colleges and the superintendent/president emeritus of Palomar College in California.

NEW DIRECTIONS FOR COMMUNITY COLLEGES • DOI: 10.1002/cc

2

As increased accountability is demanded of community colleges at the same time that state funding is being drastically cut, presidents must still maintain high standards of teaching and learning while looking for new means of fundraising. Strong support from boards of trustees is necessary for successful governance, which itself relies on effective identification and communication of educational and revenue challenges. This chapter examines some of the challenges as well as some of the avenues to success for effective governance and fundraising under these difficult circumstances.

Creating Effective Board–CEO Relationships and Fundraising to Achieve Successful Student Outcomes

Frances L. White

The Challenge

More and more accountability and successful educational outcomes are being demanded of our colleges. Achieving successful outcomes requires strong and courageous leadership at all levels of the institution, but getting the faculty to improve teaching and learning outcomes very often requires a president/chief executive officer (CEO) who not only understands the value of the teaching and learning process but also supports that process through action. Given funding limitations for faculty development and training, the president must be an advocate for both to create successful learning outcomes. The president is the sole leader in the institution who must be able to get the buy-in and support from boards of trustees to create such opportunities.

Moreover, most boards are looking at the bottom line (that is, costs) and either do not understand or give only lip service to "educational quality," facts that create an uphill effort for the president who must maintain institutional accountability, quality, and successful student outcomes. After all, it is good press for institutions to report high transfer and job placement rates, but what does it take to get the good press on transfer/job placement rates? What does a president have to be prepared to do to keep the institution focused on student achievement and academic success?

New Directions for Community Colleges, no. 156, Winter 2011 © 2011 Wiley Periodicals, Inc.
Published online in Wiley Online Library (wileyonlinelibrary.com) • DOI: 10.1002/cc.463

New presidents—indeed, all presidents—should understand why these questions and statements are significant to their personal success or failure. Personal experiences that I share in this chapter demonstrate what can be done to overcome challenges and be successful.

Create a System for Effective Governance and Board–CEO Relationships

Regardless of the culture, mission, or location of the college, certain overarching principles and considerations are common to achieving effective governance and board–president/CEO relationships (Boggs, 2006).

Many groups and individuals are involved in community college governance. In some states, such as California, the role and responsibilities of the faculty, support staff, students, and boards of trustees are mandated by legislation and statute. There are rules to be followed and honored in governance processes that lead to planning and institutional decision making. A president/CEO can hamper his or her effectiveness, as well as that of the institution, when roles, responsibilities, and rules of the road are not clearly delineated and practiced by all involved. In addition to the governance processes at the institution, the president/CEO must have an effective (functional and personal) relationship with the board of trustees. Although mutual trust and respect is at the top of the list of effective board–president/CEO relationships, so is keeping the board informed about student learning outcomes and overall student success. According to Boggs (2006), "achieving access alone is not enough; the development of a culture that places learning at the heart of the institution must have the demonstrated support of the CEO and the trustees" (p. 3).

Whether a board is elected or appointed, boards need to understand the complexity of the institution and its mission and vision for long-term planning and institutional success. It is important for the presidents/CEOs to help their boards understand their roles and responsibilities for effective oversight and governance and for the success of the college. Presidents/CEOs must inform the board through regular reports how the institution is performing to meet its mission and goals. In this process, there is opportunity for a president/CEO to share data about student success and institutional outcomes. Monitoring progress is a key function of the governing board, and it ensures accountability. By providing information and data on a regular basis, the president/CEO can help the board understand how institutional goals are being accomplished while at the same time help the board understand better what is needed to create successful outcomes. This is an opportunity that sets the stage for the president/CEO as academic leader to advocate for successful student outcomes by supporting improvements to classroom instruction and faculty development.

When I was hired as CEO at my former institution, I soon became deeply involved in the issue that student success came to some and not to others. Transfer and job placement rates were high, but because of changing student demographics at the institution, many students were failing. Open access is a strong tenet of public community colleges; thus, being able to serve more and more populations of students who are first-generation college students or those who are English-language learners and other nontraditional students poses a challenge to institutions that desire to serve all who enroll. This challenge is often met with a lack of institutional preparedness and know-how for meeting educational needs in a way that provides academic success. This was certainly the case at my institution.

As an institution, there were good people who meant well, but as we saw more students testing below college-level reading and math, we discovered a gap in how we taught and served traditional populations of students versus others. The outcomes from these differences posed a challenge for the institution; something had to be done. As the board of trustees learned more about the challenges, it gave me opportunity to introduce an innovation that would begin to reverse the problem. The innovation is mentioned later in this chapter, but because I made a practice of keeping the board informed about student success data and I had established a positive functional and personal relationship with board members, I was able to secure their support for establishing an Education Excellence Innovation Fund (EEIF) that would provide funding (through grants) to improve student success at the institution. The grants ranged from faculty development projects to projects establishing new learning communities in math, science, and English courses as well as academic support services to improve student learning and academic standing. Because of the EEIF grant opportunities, there was an expectation for innovation, and doing things the same old way was no longer a good excuse.

Promote Teaching Innovation and Successful Student Outcomes

Achieving successful student outcomes requires innovative leadership and a financial means to provide the necessary training and resources to support faculty training. Given funding limitations for faculty development in community colleges, the president/CEO must be the innovative leader and the advocate for finding alternate resources to support teaching and learning strategies that can lead to successful student outcomes.

A report from the Institute for Higher Education Leadership and Policy focuses on gaps in college access and achievement in California (Shulock and Moore, 2007). The report further reveals several serious performance problems facing the state, including:

• Preparation levels that remain comparatively low
• Low rates of college attendance among traditional-age students
• Decreasing rates of students enrolling in college directly from high school for all racial and ethnic groups

- Low rates of college completion
- Decreasing affordability
- Substantial disparities across regions and racial/ethnic populations in levels of college preparation, participation, and completion
- Projections of a large drop in the education levels of California's workforce and per capita income if the gaps among racial/ethnic groups in college going and completion persist

While the report provides policy implications for state leaders and policy makers, it brings the challenge of educating the underprepared front and center, especially for community colleges with their open-door/open-access mission. Moreover, community colleges are often the first option to provide education solutions to those who would otherwise never receive a college education.

California is facing a "skills gap" that threatens its future economy, at a time when spending on education is being cut due to a $25.4 billion shortfall in the state budget. California is ranked forty-ninth in state spending for education (when compared with other states); to make matters even worse, only 31 percent of degree-seeking community college students reach achievement (Shulock and Moore, 2010). Although the California community colleges are in a period of austerity, there is still the demand for student outcomes that lead to graduation and completion. How can an institution provide better student outcomes? How does the institution identify the resources needed to support quality teaching and learning that can lead to successful student outcomes? Promoting teaching innovation in the community college and providing the needed funding for faculty training and professional development can be a key factor in creating successful student outcomes. Again, the president/CEO must be the advocate for creating a culture of achieving successful student outcomes.

Understand Critical Pedagogy and Learning Outcomes

Today, California's policy makers and educational leaders are grappling with problems related to a skills gap, high drop-out rates among certain demographics, and low college persistence and completion rates. Currently, state public institutions award slightly more than 110,000 bachelor's degrees each year, and private institutions award 40,000. There is a projected shortfall of 1 million college graduates for 2025. According to one report, to meet the projected demand by 2025, the state would need to immediately increase the number of degrees awarded by almost 60,000 per year, about 40 percent above current levels (Johnson, 2009). Moreover, students of color, students from low incomes, and students who are the least prepared for college-level work are sometimes overlooked and are at greater risk of leaving college at the first signs of failure (Woodlief, Thomas, and Orozco, 2003).

As mentioned earlier, community colleges can play a vital role in filling the gap between high school and a four-year college or university. And certainly, the community colleges are seen as the economic engine to improve the economy by awarding degrees and certificates to a highly skilled workforce. But a renewed focus on teaching and learning in the community colleges should be implemented to improve college persistence and completion rates. If this is to be done, the community colleges' role in higher education would be well served in producing more highly skilled workers and college transfer–ready students who persist and complete at the baccalaureate level. But why don't students persist? Why don't they complete? Obviously, there is no one answer to the problem, but quality teaching and learning is at the core of a potential solution.

While academic preparedness is a good predictor of college success, the role of teachers cannot be overlooked. Richard Elmore (2006) identifies the "instructional core" as the relationships between teachers and students and the organizational practices that support those relationships. But, perhaps due to lack of training, some teachers fail to meet the needs of students (Grubb, 1999). In observations and interviews with more than 250 community college teachers, Grubb discovered that many teachers lacked the knowledge to effectively engage students. In the current literature, critical (teaching) pedagogy places emphasis on strategies that improve learning outcomes for students. Critical pedagogy is concerned with restructuring traditional teacher/student relationships so learning provides more usefulness and meaning in the learning process (Freire, 2009). Faculty professional learning and training is essential for successful pedagogical innovation. In the California community colleges, teachers are discipline-trained and typically employ teacher-centered pedagogy versus student-centered education. Students are viewed as docile receptacles "banking" information delivered from a lecture. But, in contrast to the banking approach, "problem-posing education" is a more student-centered pedagogy, and the meaningful dialogue (replacing the lecture) creates knowledge grounded in the experiences of students and teachers (Freire), ensuring successful learning and improved student outcomes. This approach embraces the notion of Elmore's (2006) "instructional core," establishing learning relationships (between teacher and student) while creating organizational practices that support the relationships. Thus, successful student learning outcomes can be achieved by employing student-centered teaching pedagogies and creating organizational practices to support student-centered learning relationships.

Most community college teachers want to teach in community colleges, and they deserve support in their efforts to bring quality teaching and learning to the classroom. However, the opportunities for faculty to get away from the chalk-and-talk lectures are usually the result of limited funding for conference travel, where they can be exposed to other teaching innovations. Unfortunately, these conferences have not been consistently supported at many college campuses in recent years, due primarily to the loss of staff development dollars previously funded by the state. College operating budgets are limited and strained, causing support for faculty training and development to go by the wayside in most cases.

Raise Funds for Faculty/Staff Development to Support Innovation

Fundraising, long the purview of private colleges, has now become common in public colleges. Fundraising programs are growing in community colleges, and as a response to constraints on college budgets, college boards and CEOs are making private fundraising a priority (Boggs, 2006).

Earlier in this chapter, I mentioned that I was able to get the support of the board to establish the EEIF at my former institution. The board established a goal for academic excellence and actually funded the goal with the objective of setting aside funds for the EEIF program. These funds were augmented by annual fundraising. Although the funds could be used for planning, they were designed primarily to help fund new approaches to teaching and learning and academic support services that improve student success.

When I was a college president and CEO, I believed in the value of student success. I understood the value of teaching and learning in general and the importance of supporting classroom instruction specifically. One way to support innovation is to pursue state and federal grants. These grants provide needed resources to address specific institutional needs toward achieving improved student learning outcomes and student success. But the grants expire, and often there is no financial backup plan to sustain a given program or innovation.

At each college where I served as president, I instituted a committee of community leaders who fundraised for a teaching and learning innovation fund at the institution. The funding program was called different names at each of the colleges, but its purpose was to provide grants to faculty and staff to dream out loud and create a learning environment where students could be successful. These innovation funding committees were very successful and were able to raise millions of dollars over the years. Although the grants were competitive, and some were not approved, many grants were awarded to faculty and staff members who created new teaching pedagogies, special programs, and academic support services that improved student success. Some of the projects that were awarded were eventually institutionalized. It is very apparent today that without these innovation funds, many faculty and staff members would not have been able to train or create new and meaningful learning experiences for their students. The additional funds kept innovation alive at both institutions, and the innovation programs continue as of this writing.

Finally, in times of fiscal constraints and scarcity, presidents must be creative in their approach to securing student success at their institution. Success in securing state or federal grants can provide a funding boost for innovation, depending on the grant. During my years serving as president and CEO, I learned that finding ways to support teaching innovation can improve student learning outcomes. The president/CEO is the sole leader in the institution who must advocate for student success, getting buy-in and support from internal constituents and the external community. Creating structures and opportunities for fundraising to promote teaching innovation can make a big difference in achieving successful student outcomes. Establishing a system for effective governance and board/CEO relations goes a long way toward achieving successful outcomes and institutional accountability.

References

Boggs, G. R. *Handbook on CEO–Board Relations and Responsibilities*. Washington, D.C.: Community College Press, 2006.

Elmore, R. F. *School Reform From the Inside Out: Policy, Practice, and Performance.* Cambridge, Mass.: Harvard Education Press, 2006.

Freire, P. *Pedagogy of the Oppressed* (30th anniversary ed.) New York: Continuum, 2009.

Grubb, N. W. *Honored But Invisible: An Inside look at Teaching in Community Colleges.* New York: Routledge, 1999.

Johnson, H. *Educating California: Choices for the Future.* San Francisco: Public Policy Institute of California, 2009.

Shulock, N., and Moore, C. *Rules of the Game: How State Policy Creates Barriers to Degree Completion and Impedes Success in California Community Colleges.* Sacramento: Institute for Higher Education Leadership, California State University, 2007.

Shulock, N., and Moore, C. *Divided We Fail: Improving Completion and Closing Racial Gaps in California's Community Colleges.* Sacramento: Institute for Higher Education Leadership, California State University, 2010.

Woodlief, B., Thomas, C., and Orozco, G. *California's Gold: Claiming the Promise of Diversity in Our Community Colleges. California Tomorrow.* Oakland, Calif.: California Tomorrow, 2003.

FRANCES L. WHITE, PhD, is retired superintendent and president emerita, Marin Community College District, Kentfield, California, and former president, Skyline College, San Bruno, California.

NEW DIRECTIONS FOR COMMUNITY COLLEGES • DOI: 10.1002/cc

The missionary zeal of community colleges in the 1960s is still needed to meet the challenges they still face today: helping underserved and underprepared students succeed, and offering a strong general education curriculum that provides the foundation and framework for later academic and professional success. Even as economic, social, and political conditions change, community colleges can and must still provide national leadership in helping more students achieve success, guiding unsuccessful students to alternatives that will allow them to be successful, and preparing students for meaningful citizenship.

The Next Community College Movement?

Charles R. Dassance

It Was the Best of Times

In the fall of 1968, having just completed my master's degree, I began my first job as a counselor in a community college in upstate New York. Although my title was counselor, I was assigned administrative responsibility for the financial aid and job placement programs. My previous experience in financial aid consisted of a ten-week practicum in the Financial Aid Office at Michigan State University as part of my graduate program. To say it was a different time in community colleges would be an understatement.

After more than forty years of working as a community college educator/administrator, the last twenty years or so as a president, I retain my love and enthusiasm for community colleges. The community college has changed in the past forty years, of course, and the future promises more change. From the vantage point of nearing the end of my full-time professional career, I have pondered what future challenges are in store for community colleges. I do so with the full realization that there is no way to predict the pressures these colleges will face but also with certainty that community colleges must continue to change to fulfill their mission.

In 1968, the United States was nearing the end of a decade of exceptional growth for community colleges. Their enrollment grew from 646,527 in 1959–60 to more than 2.5 million by the end of the decade. Enrollment growth was helped considerably by a 52 percent increase in the fourteen- to twenty-four-year age groups during the 1960s. From 412 in 1960, the number of community colleges in the United States more than doubled to 909

New Directions for Community Colleges, no. 156, Winter 2011 © 2011 Wiley Periodicals, Inc.
Published online in Wiley Online Library (wileyonlinelibrary.com) • DOI: 10.1002/cc.464

by 1970 (Witt, Wattenbarger, Gollattscheck, and Suppliger, 1994). That growth represented adding a community college a week for ten years!

The 1960s were a period of great social change in America, and community colleges were well positioned to ride that wave of change. Providing more opportunity to underserved populations in higher education fit well with the social impetus to end poverty and racial and gender inequities. The tension between meritocracy and egalitarianism, an ever-present tug and pull in American democracy, swung sharply to the side of egalitarianism. The open-door community college was regarded by many as the type of institution that embodied the social consciousness appropriate to the times.

George B. Vaughan, while serving as president of Piedmont Virginia Community College, aptly captured the mood of community college educators when he wrote an essay comparing the community college to the beacon of hope the Statute of Liberty had been for immigrants landing at Ellis Island earlier in the century (c. 1980). Many who worked in community colleges were young and embodied the spirit of missionaries, often talking about the "community college movement" as a kind of sacred calling to break down the barriers of access to higher education. It was an exhilarating time for community college educators well into the 1970s, and there is no doubt about the community college's role in helping open the doors of higher education to millions of previously underserved students.

Most of that early missionary fervor abated as community colleges matured and most of the gender, racial, and financial barriers related to access were addressed. Community colleges are in a much different place than they were fifty years ago. If they were the brash new institutions forcefully pushing aside the established order in higher education a half century ago, community colleges are now an accepted part of that established order. That is not to say that their core mission has changed significantly, but merely to observe that community colleges are no longer driven by the kind of revolutionary zeal that can occur at the beginning of societal social changes like those that manifested themselves in the 1960s.

As a mature system of higher education, one that still enrolls the greatest number of minority and low income students (Carnevale, 2009), there is still much work to be done and perhaps as much need for missionary zeal as there ever was—but with a very different focus. In this chapter, I focus on the community college mission as we enter the second decade of the new millennium and suggest issues to be addressed that warrant the kind of missionary zeal typical of an earlier time in the history of community colleges. These issues, in my opinion, relate closely with the emerging emphasis on student completion.

Mission Past

There is general agreement that the mission describes what an institution does. While discussing mission in general, it needs to be emphasized that

NEW DIRECTIONS FOR COMMUNITY COLLEGES • DOI: 10.1002/cc

there is a great deal of variation among institutions that fall under the general category of community college. Differences in size, program mix, governance, and statewide coordination are among the elements that distinguish one community college from another. Such variation is not unusual; there is at least as much variation among four-year colleges. For the purpose of this general discussion of mission, then, mission will be considered in its broad sense.

The mission of community colleges has changed significantly since the founding of Joliet Junior College in 1901. Originally created as junior colleges that provided a broad general education to students at the freshman and sophomore level to prepare them for the rigors of the university (and, from the university president's point of view, to keep them from diluting the intellectualism of higher education), community colleges expanded their mission to include vocational programs and a wide array of community service programs. In Vaughan's (1995) short history of the community college, he includes developmental education and student support services as parts of the mission. Developmental education is a large part of the educational program of most community colleges. As it is a vertical change in mission (providing an educational program at the high school level), here it is considered a regular part of the mission. Student support services, which certainly are an important aspect of what community colleges provide as well, are not considered here as a separate mission element.

By the 1960s, most community colleges addressed these general roles in their mission statement, although there was and continues to be considerable variance among these colleges regarding the emphasis each role receives. As might be expected, much has been written about the community college mission. To some, the comprehensive mission of the community college reflects the impossible goal of being "all things to all people." Cross (1985) questioned whether the community college could continue its comprehensive mission, indicating that if the comprehensive mission was maintained, "there is little doubt that priorities will have to be set and observed over the next decade" (p. 36). Twenty-five years later, it would be hard to find evidence of priority setting in regard to the comprehensive mission of the community college.

The community college mission will continue to change, a reality inherent to the nature of the basic orientation of the institution. In addition, there will likely be continuing calls for the community college to prioritize its mission elements, a more likely possibility if financial support diminishes.

Vaughan (1988) captured the reality of the ever-changing mission of the community college when he discussed the successful community college, the one that is true to its mission, as the college that "will squeeze, push and pull on the mission to make it conform to community needs" (p. 26). Comparing the mission to a balloon, Vaughn saw changing societal pressures as causing community colleges to change the shape of the balloon but not alter the core elements of the mission contained within the balloon. As one part of the mission expanded, another part of the mission was diminished.

A more important consideration than expanding or contracting the mission of the community college in the future, however, may well be refocusing on mission success as determined by the degree to which the mission is accomplished. The most significant question community colleges will deal with in the future may not be their mission—what they do—but how they carry out that mission. The outcomes of the educational experience, captured in the catchphrase "student completion agenda," will be the new focus. The remainder of this chapter suggests evolving issues community colleges will need to address.

Equality of Opportunity Just the First Step

As briefly discussed earlier, community colleges have no doubt expanded educational opportunity. They enroll the highest percentage of low-income students (Carnevale, 2009), students who are seeking economic and social mobility. Coupled with the growth of college preparatory programs to address the academic needs of underprepared students, the job for community colleges of helping these students achieve academic success remains extremely challenging.

Cohen (Cohen and others, 1971) has for many years pointed out the hollowness of using access as the measure of success for achieving educational opportunity. "Although the institution offers equality of opportunity, this does little to ensure equality of educational effects" (p. 3). Even earlier, Blocker, Plummer, and Richardson (1965) questioned the return on investment for developmental education students and called for an honest reporting of results.

This is not to say that community colleges have not struggled mightily with the challenge of helping underprepared students achieve academic success and continue to do so. Providing access to higher education for underserved groups has been a monumental accomplishment for community colleges, but there will be increasing pressure for these colleges to demonstrate their success in regard to the educational progress for such students.

One of the educational controversies of the 1960s related to the role of higher education in helping students realize their aspirations in light of the realities of their academic achievement. Clark's "The Cooling Out Function in Higher Education" (1960) caused heated discussion about the appropriateness of enrolling underprepared students who had little chance of achieving their educational goals, and many who were committed to egalitarianism, such as many community college educators, saw cooling out as just one more way to deny low-income and minority students a fair chance to be successful in higher education. Cooling out, of course, is the result of many students' inability to achieve academic success in light of their hopes and dreams for a better life.

Although there is little discussion of cooling out today, there is also no clear solution to how best to help all students who enter college academically unprepared. An exception is a recent AACC Policy Brief in which Mullen (2010) mentions the cooling-out function in relation to the need for community colleges to increase their completion rates. It is clear that many underprepared students are not successful, but does the community college role end by simply giving such students a number of chances to address their academic deficiencies and, for those who cannot do so, sending them on their way? Here lies a continuing issue for community colleges (and the nation) in the future.

While major foundations have recently directed focus to the problem of improving the success of underprepared students, there is no consensus on how best to do so. Institutions need to be honest about the resources that they will need to devote to college preparatory instruction if students are to have a realistic chance of success. A good start on the problem would be for colleges to report more publicly on their success rates with such students and to develop effective programs to divert nonsuccessful students to other alternatives. Applying the missionary zeal of our earlier time to this more difficult challenge would be wholly consistent with the core philosophy of the community college. As the "student completion agenda" becomes the national mantra for higher education, it is the right time for community colleges to lead the way on this imperative.

Transfer Is Only Part of the Transfer Function

Many students begin their pursuit of a baccalaureate degree at the community college. This was the major function of the first junior colleges and remains a significant aspect of the community college mission. While much attention is given to the transfer function, that attention generally has to do with how many students actually transfer, the acceptance of transfer credits, and the eventual success of the students who transfer to the upper division in colleges and universities. As much has been written on the topic, it is not addressed here further from these aspects. Another part of the transfer function has not received much attention of late, and it will evolve as much more important in the future: the liberal arts/general education function embedded within the transfer function.

General education is one of the most important roles of the community college. In *America's Community Colleges: The First Century*, Witt, Wattenbarger, Gollattscheck, and Suppliger (1994) noted: "Throughout the history of the community college movement . . . there has been a desire to provide individuals with an education that would enable them to become productive citizens of a democratic society" (p. 273). The authors go on to relate that role to the educational ideal described by Thomas Jefferson. They are not speaking here of "productive citizens" being ones who have the skills to succeed economically, although that is likely a part of the intent, but of fully functioning citizens—citizens who can participate fully and rationally in the democratic process.

Although the community college does not bear total responsibility, they do share responsibility for not making the general educational role more important and coherent. In her recent description of current American culture, public intellectual Susan Jacoby concluded that "America is now ill with a powerful mutant strain of intertwined ignorance, anti-rationalism, and anti-intellectualism" (Jacoby, 2008, page xx). Jacoby places part of the blame for rampant "American unreason" on the changing curriculum of elementary and secondary schools (p. 172) and on a general overemphasis in education on practical results at the near exclusion of the liberal arts.

Diane Ravitch, in her most recent book (2010), opines: "Without a comprehensive liberal arts education, our students will not be prepared for the responsibility of citizenship in a democracy, nor will they be ably equipped to make decisions based on knowledge, thoughtful debate and reason" (p. 226). Ravitch aims much of her criticism at what she considers the overemphasis on high-stakes testing as the means of improving accountability in K–12 education. One result of this misguided effort to improve education has been to decrease the liberal arts part of the curriculum. It is this curriculum, according to Ravitch, toward which reform efforts need to be directed.

The community college, which has also closely associated its mission with the ideals of American democracy, has certainly not been in the forefront of deemphasizing general education and the liberal arts. But they are part of the greater educational enterprise that has done so, and they could provide leadership in reforming and renovating general education.

Cohen and Brawer (2008), who have been studying and writing about the community college for many years, have noted the important role of general education in the community college. "A general education that leads to the ways of knowing and the common belief and language that bind society together is offered in every culture through rituals, schools and apprenticeships. The community colleges are responsible for furthering it in the United States" (p. 3). The major culprit in preventing community colleges from achieving this result, according to Cohen and Brawer, has been the move to define general education as a set of distribution requirements. That change began in earnest in America in the 1960s as a reaction to what was perceived as an overly rigid, narrowly focused approach to general education. Jacoby (2009) traces the erosion of liberal arts back further in our nation's history. She suggests that the liberal arts began to erode after World War II, when thousands of veterans entered higher education and the focus of higher education began to move toward a greater vocational emphasis.

New Directions for Community Colleges • DOI: 10.1002/cc

At this point in American history, it would be difficult to argue that there is not a strong strain of antirationalism in the country. Many factors account for that, of course, including a highly polarized political system, the twenty-four-hour news cycle, and the constant availability of opinions, most not based on relevant facts, through electronic devices. More than ever in our history, the need for citizens who can think critically, understand our democratic system of government, and be thoughtfully engaged in the democratic process is essential to our future.

As community colleges ponder the future, one very significant opportunity is in rethinking the general education function as an important aspect of the student completion agenda. There is no reason community colleges could not lead a renaissance in reconsidering the purposes of the general education function and restructuring the curriculum to ensure that students gain the knowledge and sense of common culture to be truly productive citizens. While there is no need to return to the rigidity of the previous general education approach, a general education based on a wide range of distributive requirements is clearly not serving American society well. Student completion must be undergirded with demonstrated learning outcomes, and general education should be a significant aspect of those outcomes.

Can Community Colleges Deliver?

Higher education has enjoyed an exalted place among institutions in the perception of the American public and its leaders. While other institutions in American society (Congress, the government, and so on) are held in low esteem, the feelings about American higher education have remained relatively positive. The community college, after decades of being ignored by the public media, has recently received much more attention, almost all of it positive. The Obama administration's American Graduation Initiative, references in political speeches about the value of American community colleges, and the attention Jill Biden has brought to community colleges, among other things, have all raised the visibility of the community college.

There are other forces in play, however, that raise questions about whether the positive public perception of community colleges is more fragile than we are aware. In a recent analysis of the mood of the country, Yankelovich (2009) indicated that the prevailing political trend is quite negative toward institutions and that this is a very dangerous development for our democratic process. There are reasons to be concerned that higher education, including community colleges, could become a target for public resentment in the future.

In general, much of the public support for higher education, and certainly for community colleges, comes from the perception that education is the vehicle to a better life—primarily a good job. Higher education has embraced this view and frequently links the years of additional education one receives to higher earning potential. And there is little argument that the more years of education one has, the better off one is economically.

Yankelovich's research found that 87 percent of the public believe that a college education is as important as a high school diploma was in the past and that 88 percent feel that qualified students should not be denied access to higher education because of costs. As Yankelovich (2009) says, "The heart and soul of the American core value system is that education is the royal road to middle-class status" (p. 26). If that social contract is no longer perceived as viable, due to continuing high unemployment and deleveraging of the economy, might not the "institution" of higher education begin to lose its luster? The best defense against that possibility, it seems, is greater transparency about what higher education accomplishes with its students and assuring that those students have the skills and education to be truly productive citizens.

Is the "Completion Agenda" the Next Community College Movement?

A report titled *Setting a Public Agenda for Higher Education in the States* (Davies, 2006) focused attention on the falling completion rates in America's higher education and outlined an agenda for states to follow to improve educational attainment, a recognized necessity for competing globally. The framework recommended in the report includes:

- *Preparation* (how well students are prepared for higher education and training)
- *Participation* (are there sufficient opportunities for enrolling in education beyond high school?)
- *Affordability*
- *Completion* (the progress students make in attaining degrees and certificates)
- *Benefits* (what benefits derive from an educated population?)
- *Learning* (what is known about what students actually learn?)

Community colleges are a very significant part of ensuring that the nation measures up on these indicators. The first three of these—preparedness, participation, and affordability—are ones that relate closely with the core of the underlying community college philosophy. Lower costs and access have always been important aspects of community colleges, and many community colleges are working closely with their high school partners in identifying academic deficiencies in students before they enroll.

It is the last three of the indicators—completion, benefits, and learning—where there is much work to be done. The two issues I have raised here—success of underprepared students and general education—relate directly to these issues as two prime examples of areas that demand attention.

Community colleges, which are so closely associated with the ideals of America's democracy, should provide national leadership in helping more underserved students achieve success, guiding unsuccessful students to alternatives that will allow them to be successful, and preparing students for meaningful citizenship. These issues may not be as uplifting as expanding access has been but are as important to the future of the nation. We need to rekindle the missionary zeal of the 1960s and tackle these much more difficult issues, and the completion agenda may provide the necessary impetus. I am convinced that community colleges are up to the challenge.

References

Blocker, C. E., Plummer, R. H., and Richardson, R. C., Jr. *The Two Year College: A Social Synthesis*. Englewood Cliff, N.J.: Prentice-Hall, 1965.

Carnevale, A. "Higher Education and Jobs." *Forum for the Future of Higher Education*, 2009, 38–42. Cambridge, Mass.

Clark, B. R. "The 'Cooling Out' Function in Higher Education." *American Journal of Sociology*, 1960, 65(6), 569–576.

Cohen, A., and others. *A Constant Variable*. San Francisco: Jossey-Bass, 1971.

Cohen, A. M., and Brawer, F. D. *The American Community College* (5th ed.). San Francisco: Jossey-Bass, 2008.

Cross, K. P. "Determining Mission and Priorities for the Fifth Generation." In W. L. Deegan, D. Tillery, and Associates, *Renewing the American Community College*, 34–50. San Francisco: Jossey-Bass, 1985.

Davies, G. K. *Setting a Public Agenda for Higher Education in the States*. National Collaboration for Higher Education Policy: Education Commission of the States, National Center for Higher Education Management System, National Center for Public Policy and Higher Education, 2006.

Jacoby, S. *The Age of American Unreason*. Washington, D.C.: Vintage Books, 2008.

Mullen, C. M. "Rebalancing the Mission: The Community College Completion Challenge." *AACC Policy Brief* (2010–02 PBL), 2010.

Ravitch, D. *The Death and Life of the Great American School System*. New York: Basic Books, 2010.

Vaughan, G. B. "The Community College and the American Dream." Unpublished Essay [c. 1980].

Vaughan, G. B. "The Community College Mission." *AACJC Journal*, February/March 1988, 25–27.

Vaughan, G. B. *The Community College Story*. Washington, D.C.: American Association of Community Colleges, 1995.

Witt, A. A., Wattenbarger, J. L. Gollattscheck, J. F., and Suppliger, J. E. *America's Community Colleges: The First Century*. Washington, D.C.: American Association of Community Colleges, 1994.

Yankelovich, D. "How Higher Education Is Breaking the Social Contract and What to Do about It." *Forum for the Future of Higher Education*, 2009, 25–28.

CHARLES R. DASSANCE, *PhD, is president emeritus of the College of Central Florida in Ocala.*

4

This chapter offers time-tested advice for new presidents, including how to build and maintain strong relationships with trustees, how to address the persistent concerns of student success and remediation, and how to access the college's economic condition as well as how to oversee and maintain strong funding channels.

Redefining Institutional Priorities

J. Terence Kelly

As a new community college president contemplates his or her important first steps, there are many factors to consider. Some of the most significant to me are those presented in this chapter. They are factors that contributed to the success of the Alamo Community College in Texas, substantive matters that should be considered by any new president.

The areas presented in this chapter, therefore, have been time-tested and will enhance a new college president's chances of success.

Board Retreat

An urgent item on a new president's agenda is to meet with all members of the governing board at the earliest possible moment. This is essential if the process of working together is to get off to a favorable start. It is critical for the president and the board to understand the roles each plays toward the success of the college. The preferable retreat setting is a location away from the campus, such as a convenient motel with a decent meeting room, on a weekend when all are able to attend. During this time board members and president not only get together to know one another better but review the duties, responsibilities, and limitations of the roles each person plays.

A wise choice is to employ an outside consultant, one who is an expert on the relationship between a board of governors and its president, someone well credentialed to do this work. Since a consultant is a key to the success of this endeavor, it behooves the new president and board members

New Directions for Community Colleges, no. 156, Winter 2011 © 2011 Wiley Periodicals, Inc.
Published online in Wiley Online Library (wileyonlinelibrary.com) • DOI: 10.1002/cc.465

to select this individual with utmost care. One resource available is the American Association of Community Colleges.

During the meeting a consultant should present duties of the board and of the president specifically. If disagreements occur—and they likely will—they can be worked out during this retreat to the satisfaction of all participants. This session will set the tone for the rest of the time the board and president work together. A key to the success of a new president's leadership is starting off his or her tenure with a clear understanding of both board responsibilities and his or her own duties.

It is essential that the fundamental issues between the board and the president are reviewed and agreed to. For example, the president directs all staff by hiring, promoting, and terminating; develops the budget; manages the day-to-day affairs of the institution; and communicates important matters to the board. The board has the responsibility of approving the institutional policies that govern the institution as set out by board policies, and by approving the budget. Furthermore, it must be made clear that board members can act only when in full session. Individual members have no individual authority to act.

The board does have responsibility for hiring and firing the president, and matters such as evaluations of the president should be conducted in accordance with appropriate board policies. Once both board members and the new president have a clear understanding of their overall duties and responsibilities, the president can move on to other important topics without delay in day-to-day operations.

Board members and the president should have annual retreats. Whether a consultant is required depends on the situation, but it is wise to regroup periodically and focus on such issues as mission, long-range strategic plans, goals, and student achievement.

Student Success

Student success is an ongoing crisis in American community colleges. Some 50 percent of all students who attend them, including high school graduates and those who have been out of school for a long time, are deficient in some area of reading, writing, or math. Therefore, presidents have an obligation to concentrate on this problem if for no other reason than that it is such a significant issue for our country. The nation stands at nineteenth place in math and fourteenth in science of thirty-one countries ranked by the Organisation for Economic Co-operation and Development (OECD, 2009). Declines in interpersonal and critical thinking skills must also be addressed. The time to reverse this trend is now.

In an unprecedented action by the American Association of Community Colleges at its 2010 annual convention, some of the most powerful community college organizations in the country—the Association of Community College Trustees, League for Innovation in the Community

College, the Center for Community College Engagement, Phi Beta Kappa Honorary Society, National Institute for Staff and Organizational Development, and the American Association of Community Colleges—pledged to have 50 percent more students succeed in earning degrees or certificates (AACC 2011). Speaking to the need for being more successful, these organizations collectively stated that the future of American Community Colleges rests on accomplishing this pledge.

What a new president/chancellor can do specifically is to become as familiar and as conversant as possible with remediation, and address a wide variety of community audiences as to the need for accomplishing this goal. (Of course board, faculty, and other administrators must be immediately involved and solidly behind this action.) During these community meetings the president should discuss the national high school curriculum that is being developed under the guidance of the National Governors Association and the Council of Chief State School Officers. (All but two states have agreed to this strategy.) This is an approach to say something uniformly, nationwide, about our curriculum in reading, writing, and mathematics.

Following these community meetings it is time to explain the college's position to the appropriate the state officers, chambers of commerce, civic organizations, parents of students, and whoever else needs to understand this crisis in education. The president must emphasize the current federal administration's plans to overhaul the high school curriculum by the year 2020. The amount of money and the massive changes, including the dismantling of the No Child Left Behind amendment, are part of the most concerted national educational effort ever made. Remedial programs must be examined and reexamined closely to ensure that any measures taken make significant improvements.

The key here is to be knowledgeable about the conditions required to reduce remediation, transmit that knowledge to administrators and faculty responsible for carrying out those conditions, and involve these personnel throughout. If the new president does not get the faculty on board, the college will very likely be in trouble. It is no easy assignment, but it must be done.

One of the most significant studies on remediation was Dr. Robert McCabe's (2000) report to community college decision makers about remedial education and what it means for the country. Entitled *No One to Waste*, it presents a comprehensive analysis of the most important issues facing remedial education today. It remains a primary source for community colleges trying to find their way in developmental education, and is essential reading for those who seek to be adequately informed on the subject.

There are, of course, many ways to organize an institution to address the problem of remedial work. One of the best I know is to take those faculty members who are really energetic and committed to seeing students perform better and develop a special department or unit for them, designating them as learning communities, special studies, college achievement, or some comparable term. Institutional resources and support also must be in place. Instituting such changes is not easy, but it must be done if the college is going to make more students successful.

Institutional data gained through institutional assessment instruments will be of great assistance in determining a student's placement. Such instruments must be accurate, reliable, and verifiable. Learning objectives must be in place, and the final outcome must be achievable. Student assessment instruments are critically important measures of gains in student learning, and must be as foolproof as possible. In my opinion, the most important thing a new college president can do is be a leader in this must-do arena of student achievement.

A follow-up to McCabe's national study of community college remedial education is his book *Yes We Can!*, which outlines and defines the characteristics of some of the most effective community college remediation programs. This guide for developing America's underprepared students has an extensive reference list that traces some early history of the remediation movement to the most recent significant developments.

Developmental studies simply must assume a high priority in the life of both the president and the college. There must be a standard of excellence, one that is committed to the highest outcomes of achievement possible. Students must be tracked and encouraged all the time, and their special needs must be taken into consideration. The whole enterprise must be talked about in praise for doing its very best for its students. The college must have all the elements of quality in order to be recognized as one that will provide the finest instruction any student can get. A college should be able to acclaim flexibility, one that has the student as the center of the learning experience.

How the president works with faculty is dependent on many factors. Typically some college administrators with direct responsibility for faculty will be included in decision-making. In many instances, the collective bargaining unit must be consulted, as must other internal organizations that have been in place for some time, but working with the faculty is a must. The new president must gain the confidence and support from faculty from the outset if the college is to move forward. Faculty members generally are hardworking and committed to doing exactly what any new president is trying to do. With the right encouragement, they will be the best ambassadors for the president and college.

Hundreds of books and articles discuss the subject of remedial education, and a very good place to begin is with those by Dr. McCabe. Some of the strategies that have been successful are having clearly stated objectives, using mastery learning techniques, having rigorous structure, using formative evaluations continually, using a variety of techniques that help (such as tutorial education, learning communities, and video-based components), and having college-wide support and commitment for remediation efforts.

The Achieving the Dream network (2011) is made up of a number of community colleges that are working toward improvement in student success. Currently the network is made up of more than one hundred institutions in twenty-two states serving close to 1 million students. This is a major effort that uses research data to focus on student achievement. It has careful student assessment and placement policies, innovations that work, and accurate performance measures.

This project focuses on minority and low-income students and is committed to the success of large numbers of students. The network has made tremendous policy impact statements in a number of states by concentrating its efforts toward publicizing those community colleges that do outstanding work. The members of the network concentrate on committed leadership, evidence of improved programs and services, board of trustee engagement, and systematic institutional improvement.

A number of national and state organizations are committed to Achieving the Dream objectives. This effort began in 2001 and continues today. Achieving the Dream is an example of one of the most well-known and successful remediation efforts in American community colleges.

Another prerequisite to the success of dealing with remedial students is to have an advisement system that is up to date, friendly, and available. Academic advisors must be particularly knowledgeable about financial aid for low-income students, an essential part of the picture. One key piece of legislation toward success is the expanded and popular Pell grant. While funding low income students so they may attend college is a complex issue, it must be faced with imaginative solutions in order to make these students successful.

Economic Base

Since multiple sources of college income exist, their review for accuracy becomes critical to the very health of the college: some sources may underfund the amount expected; others may not be able to meet their pledge. Accordingly, new presidents should involve the most knowledgeable people available and prepare a series of presentations and discussions on the economic conditions of the institution. At stake are both public and private funds. Consequently, it behooves the president to establish solid relationships with the most informed college people responsible for attending to this income, as well as those at the funding sources.

A brief overview of major resources typically available to a local community college is presented next.

Public Funding Sources.   The public aspect of funding should be the first thing considered, beginning with the state's allocation system. College finance people can lead this discussion. The state formula and its obligations to the college must be completely understood, with annual reviews obligatory. The figures must be correct. Many times they are not; that is why it is so important to begin here.

Often there are specific state funded allocations, and these too must be carefully reviewed. When I was in Texas, for example, the state provided a special allocation for new students and it was designated only for new campuses. Fortunately, college personnel found a miscalculation and that allocation was not received properly, which led to asking for proper reimbursement. Such oversights can occur. It is vitally important that the college receives all the funds it should, fairly and consistently.

Another college income source is local. The president and any designated college person such as a business manager needs to see what is available in the community supporting the college. In many communities, funding is based on local property taxes. Again, while these figures generally are difficult to calculate, they must be assessed correctly. Other states have no regular local contributions, but there are ways to obtain special allocations, such as going to the taxpayers. If they agree to the allocation, the college can obtain local contributions, often for specific issues for a specific period of time. These income sources vary both by payer and payee, but any resource must be reviewed and calculated correctly. City and/or county personnel should be involved when pursuing funds from these areas.

The president, and/or designee, must also make certain that all grants from the state that the college is entitled and qualified to receive have been contributed and earmarked for the right cause. All possible grants must be reviewed so that those that are appropriate can be followed up vigorously. This may take into account other departments or other specialized entities such that any performing arts, writing, or industrial/business grants can become utilized. Often, the president is made privy to such provisions and therefore should make certain that all appropriate grants are sought after.

The federal government is another important place to seek funds, and again this is an area that takes special focus and must be surveyed very carefully. Every appropriate federal program must be considered, including the financial aid areas such as Pell grants and federal loans. Further, once received, these funds have regulations that must be adhered to precisely. Any college-assigned, specialized people working in this area such as a business manager or assistant president under whose auspices these financial duties belong must be included. It is imperative that they be part of the analysis and final outcome of such a review.

The funding possibilities are almost endless, with changes made regularly. For example, President Obama has ensured that he will continue higher education access and success by restructuring and dramatically expanding college financial aid, making federal aid simpler, more reliable, and more efficient for students.

In addition, President Obama has proposed a plan to address college completion rates and to strengthen the higher education pipeline. His plan will invest in community colleges to equip a greater share of young people and adults with skills and education in higher demand for emerging industries. This is all the more reason for each new community college president to make certain that his or her college is fully involved in all federal programs that benefit students.

Tuition and fees are another well-known income source for the college. The new president needs to explore this area carefully, involving astute personnel, including students. The case for in- and out-of-district student costs, including out-of-state considerations, should be factored in along with what tuition and fees actually do for the institution.

Private Funding Sources. It is appropriate for a new president to review private foundation grants, both locally and nationally, to make certain that programs appropriate to the institution are covered. The president should ensure, for example, that people from local industries are involved and know enough about college interests to provide some support, especially for programs allied with those enterprises. Sometimes people in industry are eager to help and even pursue other businesses and industries to assist the college. Forming partnerships can be a big plus for the college. For example, the Toyota car dealership in San Antonio, Texas, made a tremendous contribution by having local colleges train their people to be efficient and to stay up to date, an opportunity that remains to this day.

A few national offices have pledged to improve community colleges. The Gates Foundation deserves maximum consideration since it has become a major contributor to community colleges. The institution should be fully involved.

The Achieving the Dream objective is also appropriate to investigate. If the college is not already involved in the program, it should become involved. As mentioned earlier, Achieving the Dream is already having a profound impact on how community colleges act in regard to student success. Wise community colleges join that movement.

The new president should explore as many funding resources as possible to make certain that the institution is where it needs to be when it comes to outside funding.

Any local foundations, private gifts, and endowment income should be explored by the president and college members as this will certainly strengthen the bonds between the college and the communities it serves. The president should ensure that there is a full review of foundation income and related gifts, all of which will make a significant difference. All college personnel should participate to make certain that important community organizations are contacted and that there is an ongoing process for soliciting endowments and the like. Often individuals within the college community are willing to provide funds for projects that pique their own personal interests.

Reviewing the financial situation of an institution is a very positive step forward. After assessing this review and setting into motion those features that will best improve what it is the college intends to do, the new president should find the institution in a better place than it was before— certainly an achievable goal.

Summary

Your community college can do better. As president, you must be outspoken on the issue of remedial education, continually talking about this problem and getting the whole institution behind making students more successful. Working closely with the board, college members, and the communities being served, there is much to be gained by finding ways to improve funding sources. It will take some time and many initiatives to find the best ways to proceed, but there is tremendous pressure on you from your college and from the large community to do better—and you will if you try earnestly.

References

Achieving the Dream. *Strategies at Achieving the Dream Colleges.* 2011. http://www.achievingthedream.org
American Association of Community Colleges. *College Completion Challenge: A Call to Action.* Washington, D.C.: 2011.
Boswell, K., and Wilson, C. D. *Keeping America's Promise: A Report on the Future of the Community College.* Denver, CO: Education Commission of the States and League for Innovation in the Community College, 2004.
Boylan, H. R., and Saxson, P. *What Works in Remediation: Lessons from 30 Years of Research.* National Center for Developmental Education, 1992.
McCabe, R. H. *No One to Waste; A Report to the Public Decision-Makers and Community College Leaders.* Washington, D.C.: American Association of Community Colleges, 2000.
McCabe, R. H. *Sewing a Seamless Education System.* Denver, CO: Education Commission of the States, 2001.
McCabe, R. H. *Yes We Can!* Phoenix, Ariz.: League for Innovation in the Community College and American Association of Community Colleges, 2003.
Moltz, D. "Community Colleges' Unfunded Mandate." *Insider Higher Ed.*, May 17, 2010. http://www.insidehighered.com/layout/set/print/news/2010/05/17/completion.
National Governors Association. "Draft K-12 Common Core State Standards Available for Comment." 2010.
Organisation for Economic Co-Operation and Development. "Education at a Glance 2009: OECD Indicators." 2009.
Peter D. Hart Research Associates Inc./Public Opinion Strategies. "Rising to the Challenge: Are High School Graduates Prepared for College and Work?: A Study of Recent High School Graduates, College Instructors, and Employers." February 2005, pp. 2–14.

J. TERENCE KELLY, EdD, is the former chancellor emeritus of Alamo Community College District, San Antonio, Texas.

NEW DIRECTIONS FOR COMMUNITY COLLEGES • DOI: 10.1002/cc

The current economic, social, and political climate presents such an unprecedented threat to the mission of community colleges that only radical changes will ensure a future in which their quality and purpose are maintained. This chapter offers a framework for how presidents and boards can meet the urgent need of staying true to the college's mission in the face of emerging fiscal and educational crises.

Increased Enrollment + Student Success – Funding = ?

James D. Tschechtelin

As the story goes, a frog dropped in a pot of boiling water will immediately jump out. However, a frog placed in a pot of tepid water will stay there as the water temperature rises until it is cooked. The coming five to ten years will drop community colleges into a lot of hot water. The question is this: Will community colleges sense the danger and jump out, or will they simply try to acclimate and get cooked? The theses of this chapter are that (1) current trends in the external environment of community colleges constitute such an unprecedented threat that their mission will inevitably be damaged, and (2) only radical changes by community colleges will secure a future in which their quality is sustained. Incremental, short-term responses are futile in the face of this new reality.

Assumptions

Two assumptions are made in this analysis. First, it is assumed that an educated citizenry is essential to a democratic and successful nation. Thomas Jefferson wrote, "If a nation expects to be ignorant and free in a state of civilization, it expects what never was and never will be." Education is important for economic growth and for the human development of our country. Education promotes economic development through the creative energy that leads to new ideas as well as to the preparation of men and women with the ability to participate fully in the knowledge-based economy. The ability of our nation to compete in a global economy depends on

New Directions for Community Colleges, no. 156, Winter 2011 © 2011 Wiley Periodicals, Inc.
Published online in Wiley Online Library (wileyonlinelibrary.com) • DOI: 10.1002/cc.466

an educated citizenry. "Our nation's dominant position in the world order is at great risk" (College Board, 2008). Education promotes human development by giving each person the opportunity to develop his or her gifts and talents to the fullest possible degree.

Second, it is assumed that community colleges are the segment of higher education that bears the greatest responsibility for educating low-income students and students of color. Community colleges provide education and training to 43 percent of the college students in the nation and to even higher proportions of low-income students and students of color (American Association of Community Colleges, 2011b).

Trends Facing Community Colleges

Three dominant forces in the external environment are shaping the new reality facing community colleges in the next decade. These forces are positioned to have a dramatic and lasting impact on community colleges. They include: growing enrollment, pressure to improve student success, and sharply declining government support.

Growing Enrollment.   Community colleges have a long, proud tradition of opening doors to college for millions of students. From the earliest days of community colleges in the United States, one of the essential elements of their mission has been student access. Community colleges have opened the doors to higher education in multiple ways, improving geographic access, financial access, academic access, and disabled access. With low tuition and open admission policies, community college enrollment had grown to 6.8 million credit students in 2007 (American Association of Community Colleges, 2011b). The American Association of Community Colleges estimates that enrollment in community colleges grew 16.9 percent between 2007 and 2009. Some of this growth can be attributed to the recession of 2008–2009; enrollment growth in community colleges is often inversely related to the strength of the economy as men and women turn to college to prepare for new or upgraded careers. Minority student enrollment in higher education is growing rapidly, and the greatest increases are in community colleges (Fry, 2010). This growing enrollment in community colleges brings pressures to hire additional faculty and staff, secure additional facilities, and provide supporting resources.

Pressure to Improve Student Success.   While student *access* has long been a theme for community colleges, more recent emphasis has been on student *success*. Earlier work on the Learning College by O'Banion (1997) set the stage, and the current accent on student success began in 2004 with a multiyear national initiative, Achieving the Dream (B. McClenney, personal communication, January 7, 2011). Spurred by data showing that only 45 percent of entering community college students earn an associate degree or transfer to a four-year college within six years, Achieving the Dream (2011) currently includes more than 130 institutions in 24 states and the District of Columbia. The purpose of Achieving the Dream is to improve the success of community college students and of low-income students of color in particular. The initiative is based on four principles: committed leadership, the use of evidence/data, broad engagement (especially faculty), and systemic institutional improvement (MDC, 2006). Colleges track results on five key variables, from the course completion rate in developmental courses to the graduation rate.

The interest in student success expanded rapidly when government officials took up the cause. In 2009, President Barack Obama announced a proposal for an American Graduation Initiative. This new proposal was aimed at increasing the number of persons with college degrees and sought an additional 5 million community college degrees and certificates by 2020 and new steps to ensure that those credentials will help graduates get ahead in their careers (American Association of Community Colleges, 2011a). The National Governors Association (2010) launched a Complete to Compete initiative, which seeks to, among other things, increase degree attainment and improve higher education productivity.

The new emphasis on student success is closely related to the theme of quality in the mission of community colleges. While quality is often cited as a part of community college mission statements, the new pressure to improve student success rates has placed additional stress on community college leaders. Some leaders have even termed this new emphasis an "unfunded mandate," as if aspiring to graduate an increasing proportion of students were a novel idea (Moltz, 2010). It is accurate to point out that additional resources are needed, but the obligation to improve graduation and transfer rates is not new. Community colleges have always had the obligation to see that every student has the best possible opportunity to succeed.

Sharply Declining Government Support. The confluence of increasing enrollment with expectations for higher rates of student success has occurred at the same time that the nation is experiencing the deepest recession since the Great Depression. Not only have tax revenues fallen dramatically, but strong political forces have opposed any increases in tax rates. As housing values have dropped, revenue from property taxes has fallen. On the other side of the ledger, government expenses for healthcare and retirement benefits have increased. In state budgets, funding for higher education is often regarded as discretionary when compared with mandated funding for major items such as K–12 schools and Medicaid. As such, higher education is frequently a target for reductions during lean economic times.

State and local funding for community colleges has been severely reduced in nearly every part of the country. Katsinas and Friedel (2010) surveyed state directors of community colleges about the status of funding and reported that twenty-two states are projecting budget cuts for their community colleges in fiscal year 2011. Among states with the greatest budget cuts are Hawaii (23 percent), Iowa (13 percent), Arizona and Massachusetts (12 percent each), and Oregon (10 percent). The United States weathered recessions in the early 1990s and the early 2000s, but in neither of those times were there proposals such as current ones to close four community colleges (Texas) or to cut state aid by one-half (Arizona). Some community college leaders go so far as to say "The truth is that the money will never come back" (Bumphus, 2010). The new reality is clearly a departure from previous recessions.

What Are the Choices for Community Colleges?

Where does this convergence of forces leave community colleges? Increasing access plus additional push for student success minus funding equals what future for community colleges? This chapter makes the case that the community college mission has been stretched beyond the breaking point in terms of sustaining access and quality and beyond the ability to serve both enrollment and student outcome goals. Something has to give. *What will be diminished, and how will those decisions be reached?* The deep reductions from state and local revenues can no longer be resolved with simple belt-tightening. Community colleges face fundamental questions.

What are the alternatives for presidents and boards of trustees? Will community colleges change their mission? What will be the impact on quality? Will presidents and boards of trustees make courageous, conscious, and strategic decisions, or will they avoid these choices and instead permit their institutions to slip quietly and incrementally, surrendering access and/or quality? This chapter provides a framework for strategic thinking, organizational change, and management that can be used by presidents and boards to meet this urgent problem.

Traditional Responses. Like the frog in a slowly heating pot of water, community colleges can and often do take incremental steps to deal with the new reality. It is the easiest thing to do. Tuition levels can be increased. Fees are created or augmented. Hiring freezes are implemented. Personnel cuts are a frequent focus, since in many community colleges, about 80 to 85 percent of unrestricted expenses are for salary and fringe benefits. A study by the Education Policy Center of actions being taken to cope with budget cuts in fiscal year 2011 reported, "Officials from 37 states predict a budget gap this fiscal year for community colleges. The most popular strategies for closing these gaps were 'across-the-board cuts,' 'deferred maintenance' and 'furloughs'" (Katsinas and Friedel, 2010, p. viii). Another frequent target for reductions is professional development, thereby sacrificing the education and training that colleges need to keep their programs and technology relevant for the future. In community colleges with negotiated budgets, one option is to reduce enrollment by reducing the number of course sections offered. However, in community colleges in states with formula-based funding, that option may not be the most prudent; state aid and tuition may cover the marginal cost of enrolling more students. The State of Washington is considering the use of Web-based instructional materials in lieu of textbooks as a way of making college more financially accessible (Overland, 2011).

Radical Thinking

> Problems cannot be solved at the same level of awareness that created them.
>
> —Albert Einstein

It is within the theses of this chapter that something has to give when colleges simultaneously experience increasing enrollment, additional emphasis on student success, and sharp declines in government funding. Something will inevitably be diminished in the process. A college that deals with this problem incrementally will suffer an erosion of access or quality; it will be the slow, sure death of the frog in increasingly hot water. What will be diminished, and how will those decisions be made and implemented? It is also the thesis of this chapter that only radical changes by community colleges will secure a future in which their quality is sustained. Three conceptual frameworks are proposed to cope with the new reality: adopt a strategic governance model, embrace a comprehensive approach to organizational change, and manage with a transformational leadership style. The first of these is likely to bring significant changes, and the other two are intended to make the change process as smooth as possible.

Adopt a Strategic Governance Model.   It is the role of community college boards of trustees to establish and support the vision and mission of the institution (Smith, 2000). The board of trustees is responsible for seeing the big picture and for developing an appropriate long-term strategic response to it. However, many boards struggle to focus on information about major trends and chart a course through the white water of the new reality. Are most community college boards prepared for the task? Chait, Ryan, and Taylor (2005) describe widespread disappointment with the performance of boards: "There is no question that the nonprofit sector has a board problem. Frustration with boards is so chronic and widespread that *board* and *troubled board* have become almost interchangeable" (p. 11). Carver and Carver (2010) concluded that most nonprofit boards are ineffective: "Ninety-five percent are not doing what they are legally, morally, and ethically supposed to do" (p. 2).

Chait, Ryan, and Taylor (2005) propose that boards need to expand from their traditional fiduciary role to a strategic governance model and, ultimately, to a generative role in governing. In their fiduciary role, boards of trustees see their main purpose as the stewardship of assets and their main role as that of sentinel. The board monitors the work of the president. The central question for fiduciary board governance is: What is wrong?

The fiduciary role of the board is important and has to be discharged properly. However, the larger responsibility of the board must include strategic governance. In their strategic governance role, boards see their main purpose as a strategic partnership with the president and staff, and their main role as that of strategist. The central question for the board in strategic governance is: What is the plan? The partnership between the board and the president is meant to include extensive and meaningful collaboration; it does not mean a brief discussion by the board, followed by approval of what the president presents to them. When operating in a strategic role, boards and presidents have courageous conversations, asking such fundamental questions as:

- What is the mission of the college? What are the *core* elements of the mission?
- What programs are most central to the mission? What is the order of importance of elements of the mission of the college? For example, is community service more important than continuing education? Is the credit program more important than the noncredit program? Where do programs for business and industry rank in relation to transfer programs? What is the importance of outreach to local high schools?
- What is quality, and how is it best measured? How will the college know when quality is enhanced or eroded: In instruction? In academic advising? In library services? In instructional technology?
- What instructional locations are most crucial? What are the cost and the value of each branch campus or off-campus center?
- How is student financial access best measured: in relation to the median family income in the service area? In relation to the federally defined poverty threshold? In relation to the cost of public four-year education? What has been the trend in tuition and fees at the college, and at what point would the college no longer be able to claim financial access as a part of the mission?

These are not easy questions to answer, and because they concern the fundamental direction of the college, they can be expected to raise the level of tension within the college and among its external stakeholders. Traditionally, boards and presidents have maintained that the college *has* to perform all of the evolved elements of the mission and contended that the many parts of the mission support each other. That luxury is no longer possible for many community colleges if quality is to be assured.

Embrace a Comprehensive Approach to Organizational Change. Simultaneous with the board of trustees developing a clear direction for the college, how do community colleges best set out to make that change happen? At many colleges, the change process is episodic and buffeted by competing priorities. Distractions from short-term issues and day-to-day crises abound. The second framework that can help colleges deal with the new reality is to have a comprehensive, well-established conceptual and operational model for implementing the changes that are needed. Kotter (1996, 2002) provides a model based on studies done at a wide variety of organizations. At the operational level, his work on the change process (1996) outlines an eight-step process. The process is relatively linear, and a failure to achieve success in an early step can easily derail accomplishment in a subsequent step. These steps are:

1. *Establish a sense of urgency.* The change process begins by developing a strong drive among a large cadre of faculty and staff that they need to move on the problem and get something done. The central point is that people come to feel a need for *action.*

2. *Create a guiding coalition.* A small group of people with the authority, reputations, skills, and credibility are assembled to plan the change initiative. This coalition can work from a charge given to them by the board of trustees and the president.

3. *Develop a vision and strategy.* The guiding coalition develops a simple vision and sensible strategies that inspire the faculty and staff.

4. *Communicate the change vision.* The vision and strategy need to be explained effectively and explained again far and wide in the college and the community it serves. Numerous opportunities are provided for faculty, staff, and administrators to discuss the vision and strategy. The goal is to secure an emotional commitment from everyone at the college. The use of symbols in repeated and creative ways is important.

5. *Empower broad-based action.* Mostly by removing barriers to action, faculty, administrators, and staff are given the ability to act on the vision. This step can involve improvements in information systems, building of self-confidence, and even removal of administrators who disempower their associates.

6. *Generate short-term wins.* Given that the changes sought take some time to achieve, it is important that the college faculty, administrators, and staff have some tangible evidence that their commitment and new approaches are paying off.

7. *Consolidate gains and produce more change.* Changes are linked so that additional changes are built on each other and momentum is not lost. The hazard is that energy will fade and people will lose interest in the vision.

8. *Anchor new approaches in the culture.* The changes become enduring through changes in the faculty and staff norms. The "way we do things around here" becomes oriented to elements originally designed in the vision. Careful selection of new hires, fitting promotions, and faculty and staff development programs can help to cement the new culture being sought.

Kotter's approach at the conceptual level regarding change is clear but not mechanical. He stresses the importance of leadership and underscores the emotive component in the change process. He writes:

The single most important message . . . is very simple. People change what they do less because they are given an *analysis* that shifts their *thinking* than because they are *shown* a truth that affects their *feelings.* (2002, p. 1).

Our main finding, put simply, is that the central issue is never strategy, structure, culture, or systems. All those elements, and others, are important. But the core of the matter is always about changing the behavior of people, and behavior change happens in highly successful situations mostly by speaking to people's feelings. This is true even in organizations that are very focused on analysis and quantitative measurement, even among people who think of themselves as smart in an M.B.A. sense. (2002, p. x)

Orchestrating a successful change process is a difficult enterprise, as individuals and groups resist the new direction and short-term crises emerge. One way for the college to maintain a sense of focus on the most important goal is to employ a consultant with knowledge and experience in governance and change. The college can benefit from someone with an external point of reference who can help to keep the entire initiative on track. Achieving the Dream has employed this approach successfully, with a coach and data facilitator assigned to each college who make periodic visits to the campus (MDC, 2006). These two consultants begin with three two-day visits per year at the onset and two visits per year in subsequent years. A study of Achieving the Dream work in Massachusetts found the contributions of the consultants to be valuable. "Among the supports provided by Achieving the Dream, coaching and data facilitation were repeatedly cited among interviewees as the most significant contributors to colleges' progress under the initiative" (Pauley and Torres, 2010, p. 14).

Manage with Transformational Leadership Style.   The first two parts for an effective response to the new reality for community colleges are to adopt a strategic governance model and to embrace a comprehensive approach to organizational change. Those elements pose significant departures from business as usual and require the development of an atmosphere that will support the changes being made. Hence, the third framework for dealing with the new reality is for the college to manage with a transformational leadership style that will provide a climate of openness, trust, and concern for individuals. In a study of leadership that began with 296 community college chief executive officers (later distilled to a group of 50), Roueche, Baker, and Rose (1989) extracted a list of five themes that characterize transformational leaders. Bass (1985) and Yukl (2011) also describe transformational leadership.

The first of the five themes is *vision.* A transformational leader helps to shape the vision of the college in partnership with the board of trustees and in consultation with the faculty and staff. There needs to be an overarching and inspiring sense of where the college is going. This theme reinforces a similar step in Kotter's change process (1996).

Influence orientation is the second theme. It is "the process of shared attention to problems and understanding of roles to be played in resolution. Generally, it results in increased power delegation and empowerment, promoting self-actualization of both leaders and followers" (Roueche, Baker, and Rose, 1989, p. 264).

The third theme is *people orientation*: Leaders value individuals as well as the contributions of teams in the college. There is a tone of concern for students and their success as well as each faculty, administrator, and staff member. Emphasis on student success will undergird the external pressure for improved student success with a positive internal college motivation.

Transformational leaders establish and sustain a *Motivational Orientation*, the fourth theme. In this theme, "[f]ollowers are motivated to achieve and are excited through performance and results" (Roueche, Baker, and Rose, 1989, p. 272). Working with this perspective, faculty, administrators, and staff use their talents more creatively.

Values orientation is the fifth theme of transformational leadership. Leaders need to model high standards of integrity, commitment, and ethical behavior. This theme is absolutely necessary to gain the respect of the faculty and staff. In times of great change at the college, suspicion and cynicism about the motives and intentions of leaders can accelerate. The values orientation must be well established before dramatic changes are discussed and implemented.

Summary and Conclusions

A new reality in the external environment of community colleges poses an urgent and significant challenge. There is pressure for increased student access plus new stress on increasing student success; both come during a time when government funding is sharply declining. The theses of this chapter were that (1) current trends in the external environment of community colleges constitute such an unprecedented threat that their mission will inevitably be damaged, and (2) only radical changes by community colleges will secure a future in which their quality is sustained. Incremental, short-term responses are futile in the face of this new reality. At substantially lower levels of funding, community colleges cannot do everything that they once did.

Because of the importance of education to the national interest and the central role played by community colleges both nationally and locally, it is critically important that community colleges respond in a way that best serves students and the country. The question becomes: What will be diminished, and how will those decisions be made? Community colleges need to take a strong, proactive approach. A framework of theories is proposed to help community colleges not only survive but succeed. Four conclusions emerge:

1. *Adopt a strategic governance model, where the board of trustees and the president work in a strong and active partnership to ask fundamental*

questions about the direction of the college. The board of trustees and the president must shape the vision of the college in the context of the big picture. The strategic governance model by Chait, Ryan, and Taylor (2005) is an excellent framework for this task.

2. *Embrace a comprehensive approach to organizational change that maps out a clear philosophy and process for coping with revisions to the directions and operations of the college.* Kotter's (1996, 2002) framework for organizational change, with its clear eight-step process and a see-feel-change (versus analysis-think-change) philosophy, would be outstanding for this activity.

3. *Manage with a transformational leadership style.* In this element, the president and the administrators strive to establish a positive and supportive atmosphere, where every person in the college feels that he or she is a valued and respected part of the institution. Roueche, Baker, and Rose's (1989) model of transformational leadership is an ideal framework for this effort.

4. *Employ a competent consultant on a long-term basis to facilitate this work.* Dealing with what often seems to be perpetual white water is a daunting task, with a wide variety of day-to-day issues competing for attention. By hiring a consultant with knowledge and experience about governance and change, the college can benefit from someone with an external point of reference who can help to keep the entire initiative on track. Achieving the Dream has employed this approach successfully, with a coach and data facilitator assigned to each college, consultants who make periodic visits to the campus (MDC, 2006).

Is the "golden era" over for community colleges in the United States? It is possible for community colleges to emerge from the new external reality in a strong position. Community colleges do not have to muddle through; rather they can engage in a thoughtful process toward a renewed institution. The process will lead to a changed college, but it can be a strong one. It will depend on the courage and creativeness of community college boards and presidents. The frog does *not* need to cook as the water temperature rises.

References

Achieving the Dream. 2011. http://www.achievingthedream.org/.

American Association for Community Colleges. (2011a). "The American Graduation Initiative: Stronger American Skills through Community Colleges." http://www.aacc.nche.edu/Advocacy/aginitiative/Pages/obamafactsheet.aspx.

American Association for Community Colleges. (2011b). "Fast Facts." http://www.aacc.nche.edu/AboutCC/Pages/fastfacts.aspx.

Bass, B. M. *Leadership and Performance Beyond Expectations.* New York: Free Press, 1985.

Bumphus, W. G. Interview by J. Gonzalez, *Chronicle of Higher Education.* 2010, December 5. http://chronicle.com/article/Incoming-Leader-of/125598/?sid=cc&utm_source=cc&utm_medium=en.

Carver, J., and Carver, M. "Carver's Policy Governance Model in Nonprofit Organizations." 2010. http://www.carvergovernance.com/pg-np.htm.

Chait, R. P., Ryan, W. P., and Taylor, B. E. *Governance as Leadership.* Hoboken, N.J.: John Wiley & Sons, 2005.

College Board. *Coming to Our Senses: Education and the American Future.* New York: Author, 2008.

Fry, R. *Minorities and the Recession-era College Boom.* Washington, DC: Pew Research Center. 2010. http://pewsocialtrends.org/2010/06/16/minorities-and-the-recession-era-college-enrollment-boom/.

Katsinas, S. G., and Friedel, J. N. *Uncertain Recovery: Access and Funding Issues in Public Higher Education.* Tuscaloosa, AL: University of Alabama Education Policy Center, 2010.

Kotter, J. P. *Leading Change.* Boston: Harvard Business School Press, 1996.

Kotter, J. P. *The Heart of Change.* Boston: Harvard Business School Press, 2002.

MDC. "Increasing Student Success at Community Colleges." Chapel Hill, NC: MDC, Inc., 2006. http://www.achievingthedream.org/_images/_index03/Framing-Paper-July-2006-final.pdf.

Moltz, D. "Community Colleges' Unfunded Mandate." *Inside Higher Ed.,* 2010, May 17. http://www.insidehighered.com.

National Governors Association. *Complete to Compete.* Washington, DC: Author, 2010. http://www.nga.org/Files/live/sites/nga/files/pdf/10gregoirebrochure.pdf.

O'Banion, T. *A Learning College for the 21st Century.* Phoenix, Ariz.: American Council on Education/Oryx Press Series on Higher Education, 1997.

Overland, M. A. "State of Washington to Offer Online Materials as Texts." *Chronicle of Higher Education,* 2011, January 11. http://chronicle.com.

Pauley, E., and Torres, N. *Massachusetts Achieving the Dream Phase 1 Findings and Recommendations.* New York: MDRC, 2010.

Roueche, J. E., Baker III, G. A., and Rose, R. R. *Shared Vision: Transformational Leadership in American Community Colleges.* Washington, DC: American Association for Community Colleges, 1989.

Smith, C. J. *Trusteeship in Community Colleges.* Washington, DC: Association of Community College Trustees, 2000.

Yukl, G. *Leadership in Organizations* (7th ed.). Upper Saddle River, N.J.: Prentice-Hall, 2011.

JAMES D. TSCHECHTELIN, EdD, *is an adjunct professor at the Graduate School of Management and Technology, University of Maryland University College; coach to Achieving the Dream; and retired president of Baltimore City Community College, Baltimore, Maryland.*

6

As fiscal, accountability, and enrollment pressures rise, community college presidents need to work more closely and effectively with elected officials at the local, state, and federal levels in order to advocate for their schools and students. Colleges will be expected to carry an even greater burden in meeting demands for both increased student enrollment and student success, and they must have demonstrable results and effectively persuasive data and stories to show legislators and other funders in order to keep them attentive to the needs and value of community colleges.

Giving Voice: Advocating for the Community College

Mary Ellen Duncan, Calvin Ball

Presidents need to be better than ever before in making the case for support at the local, state, and federal governmental levels. Daniel Phelan wrote in 2005 that "[p]residents, chancellors, and other campus leaders face what seems like an ever-increasing number of fiscal pressures as they seek to meet the expanding needs of their constituencies while balancing a stressed budget" (p. 87). This statement is far truer today than it has ever been, for a number of reasons: There are fewer resources available from governmental sources; there are more students to serve; and there are more defined expectations for student certificate and degree completion. Presidents need to make their advocacy efforts effective, continuous, and comprehensive.

Advocacy is more than pleading or arguing a case for support of the mission and goals of community colleges; it is the art of effective communication and relationship building. Furthermore, the president has to understand the community networks that can support his or her advocacy efforts and be able to utilize those networks effectively.

While community college presidents have always had to defend various components of their mission, a stressful economic environment makes it more imperative. They must also conduct an intense review of the effectiveness of the way public dollars and tuition dollars are expended by asking, for example:

New Directions for Community Colleges, no. 156, Winter 2011 © 2011 Wiley Periodicals, Inc.
Published online in Wiley Online Library (wileyonlinelibrary.com) • DOI: 10.1002/cc.467

- Are students succeeding in developmental courses?
- Are students completing degrees and certificates?
- Is the institution addressing the needs of the students and the community?
- Are partnerships yielding results?
- Does the college change strategies when results are not adequate or improving year to year?
- Are students transferring or meeting other educational goals?

President Obama wants to focus on regaining the United States' place in the world as having the highest proportion of college graduates by 2020. Additionally, he does not hesitate to speak about the importance of community colleges, frequently visiting campuses around the country. While the attention given to community colleges is a long-awaited change, the colleges can no longer be content to give reasons why students do not graduate or transfer or get appropriate jobs. Instead, they must show continuous movement toward measurable goals in order to maintain the attention of legislators and other funders. Community college leaders also need to communicate what role their institutions play in economic development. Community colleges need resources to attain these ambitious goals, but they also need to show evidence that these resources will be used to achieve better performance results and how community colleges offer a return on investment.

Accountability is one of the pillars of effective advocacy. If colleges can show results (and not blame other segments of education), they are more likely to build respect and support among elected officials and community leaders. As competition for students increases, learners are becoming more savvy and assertive. Thus, accountability plays an important role in recruitment and retention of students who are looking for results and expect community colleges to deliver those results.

Protecting the Mission

Advocacy requires a passion, a sincere belief in the college's mission. One element of the mission that is at risk in this environment is the "open access" component. Along with the necessity to be accountable and to be transparent about the challenges faced by educating community college students, protecting the very foundation of the community college mission is another critical piece of the advocacy agenda. Community colleges need to continue to expand open access to underserved and unserved populations. Reaching such groups of people will test the creativity and problem-solving skills of community college educators. Yet the success of the U.S. economy and the strength of the U.S. democracy are dependent on educating people and preparing them to sustain themselves and their families. Harbour and Day (2009) contend that community colleges need to be more explicit in affirming their role "in educating an adult population capable of supporting a democratic society" (p. 7).

Another key element is workforce development. As communities within our nation struggle through challenging fiscal times, job creation and workforce development have been increasingly vital to success. Engrained in the mission of the comprehensive community college is this key workforce development component, which is at the forefront of many constituencies.

Students Tell the Stories Best

The president needs the facts and figures to make the case for support, but nothing is more moving than to hear the story from a student's perspective. On one occasion, when I (Duncan) was president of Howard Community College, a group of students accompanied me to the state senate budget hearings. The senator chairing the committee interrupted my testimony and asked me to let the students introduce themselves. Without any prompting or preparation, one student introduced herself, named the program she was studying, and added: "I actually get to take two classes at the same time since the wall of the trailer where we take our classes allows me to hear the lecture in the adjoining room as well." That certainly made the case for the classroom building we needed without me adding a word.

On another occasion I (Duncan) had presented several pages of student stories, each with a picture and a description of the student's field of study and goals upon graduation. Again a state senator gravitated toward those easy-to-read stories, ignoring the facts and figures I brought to make the case. "These are the real stories of real people," she said. "I am moved by this." Mary Spilde, former chair of the board of the American Association of Community Colleges, commented that

> a good story is grounded in passion and commitment, which means we need to discover what we care about individually and collectively. . . . Community colleges can always make a difference in people's lives, particularly when people come to us wounded or convinced they will fail. . . . Listen to students—from their stories construct a compelling, coherent message. (2010, p. 6)

These students are not only more "evidence" of success, they are voters who, along with the voice of community college leaders, help ensure that the case is heard.

Responding to Business Needs Is a Compelling Story Too

Another important story is the story that businesses can tell. The mini–case studies that can be written about both credit and noncredit programs that are responsive to the economic development needs of the college's service area are especially convincing. They can show how:

- Training prepared workers for job vacancies
- Training kept employees up to date so that they remained competitive and employable
- The college created new courses or programs (credit and noncredit) that responded to new or expanding industries

Many colleges have completed economic impact studies to demonstrate how the investment of state and local resources is returned at a greater rate than the original investment. But again, naming the specific companies that benefited from the investment of public and tuition dollars is a more memorable story than that complex data in an impact study. Additionally, partnering with economic development leaders can help give another set of compelling data as well as a "face" that may not be traditionally associated with the halls of academia. This other face or voice allows community college leaders the ability to convey the story of other business leaders, in their own language, hence allowing current and future supporters to hear the case that needs to be made.

Working in a Competitive Environment

From the president's perspective: Educating community college students affects the success of the entire community and relieves stress on other county and state agencies in difficult times.

From the legislator's perspective: The pre-K–12 system often appears to offer the most promise in positively impacting a society, and the four-year university seems to be the ideal vehicle for higher education.

With so many competing priorities facing elected officials, the community college president must be aware of other needs in the community. He or she starts by understanding and accepting the legislator's perspective. Again, when I was president of Howard Community College, a legislator told me that his priority was to improve a playground of an elementary school where his children went to school rather than the college's dilapidated gym. The best strategy for me was to acknowledge that need and ask him to consider a visit to the college's facility. During this visit, he began to pull off the siding in the gym and was appalled by its condition. The needed funding for the renovation was approved.

One way to increase the college's stature in the community is to develop a close working relationship with local nonprofits. For example, when possible, colleges can provide space for those nonprofits that can offer services for their students. If the college avoids the temptation to duplicate services and makes every attempt to align with compatible services for students, officials will realize that the college is concerned about the community as a whole. Often these relationships make it easier to get grant and other funding, which reward collaboration and cost effectiveness. For example, the headquarters of the Mediation and Conflict Resolution Center moved to Howard Community College, prompting the development of courses and articulation agreements with a university that supported a major in this area.

Developing Relationships

From the president's perspective: Why don't our elected officials attend more of the college functions?

From the legislator's perspective: We have hundreds of functions around the community to attend. Why doesn't the college expect us to attend fewer, meaningful functions?

The president, along with a board member and a staff member, ought to begin a relationship by a visit to the elected official. Background research should be completed prior to the visit to determine personal as well as professional ways to relate to each other. This initial visit should conclude with an invitation to visit the college for a tour conducted by a student ambassador and the president and a staff member (one who has responsibility for legislative relations). Additional invitations for key events should be sent throughout the year. When elected officials attend, they should be introduced to the attendees and given an opportunity to speak.

It is too late to begin a relationship when the legislative sessions or the budget hearings have begun. This relationship is not unlike many others. It is not built in a day, and it is the little things that really mean the most. Remembering personal details that the legislator shares about hobbies, career goals, and family facilitates relationship building. One very visible and looming role this political leader plays is as an elected official. Campaigns cost money and are won by votes.

There are different board beliefs about whether presidents should attend or contribute to the fundraisers of elected officials. Some boards forbid the involvement of presidents in any political activity. This is probably the safest strategy to be sure that one is not on the wrong side of the person elected, putting the college's requests at risk. In cases where presidents are permitted to attend fundraisers, they have to attend *all* of them, not just the candidates of one party.

Personal notes recognizing the accomplishment and support of various officials and their family members can keep the relationship vibrant and interactive on issues beyond the college's priorities. The child who makes the all-star team or the spouse who serves on a philanthropic board should be noted when appropriate.

Effective Communication

From the president's perspective: I want to tell the whole story, give all the facts—it's going to take more than the allotted two minutes.

From the legislator's perspective: I have thousands of constituents and hundreds of people asking for money and help. If I want to know your story and the facts, I will ask someone I trust.

At one budget hearing, in a year of making cuts, one president started her comments by saying that a proposed cut was "ill advised." Those of us in the audience could see the blood boiling in the members of the committee listening to our testimony. Starting with a criticism is a good way to be sure that nothing said after that will be heard. Even though more and more of our elected officials have firsthand experience with community colleges (and more of them are willing to admit it), presidents cannot make that assumption. Therefore, the brief and focused remarks presidents make in testimony need to conform to this checklist:

- Make very brief remarks, with backup data submitted in writing using illustrative graphs and charts that cite from where those data are derived.
- Focus on two or three priorities. (One is better.)
- Drape requests around the mission and the role the college plays in the community.
- Recognize verbally that the legislators have difficult decisions to make with limited resources. (What can the college bring to the table? What can the college do to make the legislator look good?)

In budget hearings in state legislatures, testimony from community colleges may follow testimony from universities. The testimony given by these individuals might not be the best models (unless the budget hearing chairman is a graduate of that university!). Often the "ego" becomes the center of attention, but that might not be enough to get the commitment the college needs.

While community colleges probably should avoid comparing their return on investment or their cost per full-time equivalent, it certainly would not hurt to show officials some of the differences in costs between universities and community colleges. In fact, in some states, private institutions get state support. Community colleges work in an open admissions environment—a more challenging task to begin with—their employees get paid less, and their students do not get the same level of resources. Recently an article in the *Baltimore Sun* reported on a bonus of over $400,000 for a university dean (Schreiber, 2010). Salaries of most community college presidents do not approach the size of that bonus.

Work with Colleagues in Your State

From the president's perspective: I know we all need capital funds, but I want to be sure our project is funded.

From the legislator's perspective: It's easy to pick favorite institutions or projects based on my background and experience. However, that might not be the right project at the right time for the right institution.

Working with others has pluses and minuses. It may mean that a particular college has to wait longer to get the project it wants but that eventually all the projects will be addressed. If a president acts outside of his colleagues, it may work only one time. After that, others will use all their clout to be sure that the outlier goes to the bottom of the list in the future. There are positive examples of united voices that leverage their human and other resources to achieve success not otherwise possible. For instance, in the early part of this century, Maryland president and trustees worked together to double the size of capital funding. Prior to that time it had been $30 million for 16 colleges.

Get Others Involved

Presidents do not usually need large numbers of supporters for their priorities, but they need the "right" supporters—people who are respected in the community. This would include board members, foundation board members, business leaders, and major donors to the college and the campaigns of legislators.

The college needs to supply a focused message for such people to use as talking points. A generic message of "We love the college" will not be sufficient to make the case.

Hire a Person or Designate Part of a Person's Job as Legislative Relations.   Without a doubt, the president needs a person to assist with legislative relations. The responsibilities of this person should include:

- Tracking the issues important to each elected official who can have an impact on the college
- Investigating the relationships between college and foundation board members and major donors to those elected officials
- Knowing the friends of elected officials, the officials' interests, and the major contributors to their campaigns
- Being responsive to any requests that come from staff or legislators, especially concerns expressed by their constituents
- Developing relationships with staff and providing detailed information for proposed legislation
- Knowing the college staff members who are experts on certain legislation, such as financial aid or TRIO programs, and using their knowledge to prepare testimony

Making the Case at the Federal Level.   Community colleges have two organizations that develop legislative priorities in cooperation with each other: the Association of Community College Trustees (www.acct.org) and the American Association of Community Colleges (www.aacc.nche .edu). Each February they hold a conference in the District of Columbia to roll out their priorities; invite key legislators to address the audience of trustees, presidents, and legislative relations staff; and encourage attendees to visit their elected officials on the Hill.

One of the major issues is always financial aid for students. Federal officials should have evidence to understand not only the need but also the return on their investment of those vital dollars.

Making the Case at the State Level.   One legislator recently commented that he never saw community college presidents at the state capital, but he did see the staff members who represented universities and occasionally university presidents. Of course, many community colleges do not designate a staff person to take on legislative relations, but perhaps they should. If community college leaders were to have frequent conversations about the college with legislators, they would have less need to say everything at once.

In Maryland, when the trustees worked together on behalf of their colleges, capital dollars were first doubled and then tripled. Working together at the state level makes a difference, but someone has to take the lead, either a president or a trustee.

Some colleges have board committees that develop plans, along with college staff. Such plans include the following components:

- Funding priorities
- Key legislative decision makers
- Message
- Deployment of staff, trustees, students, others to carry the message

> Community colleges face fierce competition for the attention of state and local legislators and policymakers, and the competition for more public dollars is especially fierce. . . . Effective advocacy at the state level requires knowing the issues, being armed with good information, getting to know your legislators and making yourself and your college known to them, staying in touch with them and, at the appropriate time, making a clear, cogent statement on the policy or legislation in question and requesting their support. (Association of Community College Trustees, 2009, p. 36)

Some states have central offices for their community colleges that take the lead in legislative relations. Chancellor Glenn DuBois of the Virginia Community College System commented, "I don't go in talking about what our system needs. Rather, I tell them about what we provide for the state and its citizens. I talk to them about the value we add for the state" (Kazis, 2006, p. 50).

Describing the value that community colleges add should include data relevant to the role legislators envision for themselves. Those data need to come alive by putting a face on the people who benefit.

Making the Case at the Local Level.   At the local level, often there are fewer people with whom to meet. Conversely, it is easy for a community college leader to fall into the trap of neglecting the locally elected official for the state or federal office holder. Local elected officials are often close to their constituencies. Many times they are the first line of defense when it comes to issues surrounding education, workforce development, and quality of life. For that reason, it is advisable to connect with local officials regarding key initiatives that align the mission of the community college with that of the local government. Locally elected officials often can influence state and federal officials as well.

Trustees are a critical asset in effective community college advocacy because they live in the community and have closer relationships with the local mayor or council person than the U.S. Senator.

In South Carolina, one of the presidents of a large college prepared a detailed list of contacts that needed to be made to get support for the construction of a new campus in a suburb. This list included dates with names of people (trustees, donors, and friends) who needed to make the contact and spanned several months prior to the time when budget decisions needed to be made. Another president of a smaller college made sure that she interacted socially with local officials year round so that her issues were familiar to them long before the deadlines were reached for budget decision making. Their efforts provided important successes year after year as a result of their diligence.

Election Year

Every two years is a great opportunity not only to educate but also to empower students in the political process. Part of that empowerment is connecting students with their representatives. That connection puts a face on the advocacy and helps add texture to the advocacy efforts in which the college engages outside of election season. Additionally, helping students articulate thoughts, needs, and their perspective leading up to and inside the voting booth reminds the elected officials for whom they work.

Practical ways to explore this opportunity include:

- Registration and Get Out the Vote activities around campus and with student groups.
- Hosting or cohosting forums with other community organizations. Doing this can serve the institutions multiple ways with both elected officials and community organizations.
- Mock voting. Practicing using ballots and machines helps demystify the election process and builds anticipation for election day.

What Not to Do

Institutional needs must supersede current political battles or the requests of individual people, including elected officials and their friends who may try to influence, bribe, or threaten presidents. Sometimes those bribes may benefit the college but put the president at risk because the request requires a behavior outside the law.

NEW DIRECTIONS FOR COMMUNITY COLLEGES • DOI: 10.1002/cc

There are numerous cases of presidents being co-opted by elected officials or people who are running for election. This is the beginning of the end of the tenure of a president. Sometimes presidents are threatened by elected officials to hire a friend or make a comment in support of their agenda. If a president thinks it is more important to preserve his or her job, this risk is only a temporary fix. Sometimes board members may ask presidents to do a favor for an elected official. This is also a risky proposition that can become very problematic for a president's tenure. Sometimes it is better to ask if the board member or elected official expects the president to resign if the request is not heeded. Doing so puts the burden (and risk) of explaining the resignation (if that is what is expected) on the person requesting the favor instead of the president. Recently a former president had to pay a $30,000 fine for contributing to a campaign of an elected official from the college's foundation. Even though the president thought he was doing something for the good of the college, he was liable for breaking the law and had to pay the price.

Board Policies

The community college president is the face of the institution and consequently carries the weight of the office and college with each appearance or gesture of support. The president, any of his or her senior staff, and those on the board share the same responsibility.

Creating official policies that prohibit administrators from attending political fundraisers fosters a face of neutrality and protects the image of the president and the college.

Many boards develop an annual legislative relations plan with roles for students, trustees, employees, and others. This keeps the advocacy agenda in front of the board all year long.

If board members decide to run for political office, it is hoped that they can be encouraged to take a leave of absence from the college board. One college reported that a board member running for office would show up at the print shop asking for his campaign materials to be reproduced. The print shop manager was between a rock and a hard place about such a request—a request that the president did not know about. When it came to the board's attention that this had happened, the board added words to its by-laws to prevent members from staying on the board while campaigning for an elected office (other than as a board member).

Role of Students

Students deserve an active role in the advocacy process. This is their chance not only to speak their voice but also learn political skills and develop public service relationships that may impact the rest of their lives. The unrehearsed contributions of students add a dimension and a convincing argument that cannot be duplicated by staff.

Communicate Legislative Priorities

The purpose of communications should be threefold: learn, educate, and persuade. The audience includes many constituencies who speak many languages, such as legislators, alumni, current and potential students, the surrounding community, businesses, and nonprofits. These languages include not just English, Spanish, Chinese, and the like; they include the vernacular conveyed through text messages, social media, and other nonconventional methodologies. When developing an effective communication strategy, a series of questions needs to be asked that includes:

- What is the purpose?
- Who is the audience and by what method is this audience best reached?
- What is the time frame?
- What is the cost?
- What is the likelihood that an investment in a communication strategy (a) yields a positive result, (b) yields the expected return on investment, and (c) can be justified to the public?

As we continue to serve in times of greater scrutiny and competition, the ability to advocate for the community college mission and to make an effective case to multiple constituencies is a requirement for current and emerging community college leaders. The community college leader can capitalize on the increased recognition of the importance of the community college but take nothing for granted as colleagues in universities often do. Community colleges must build on a culture of evidence and accountability and continue to serve those constituents who might otherwise be without access to education and jobs. Effective advocacy transcends pleas, builds on relationships, demonstrates the college's effectiveness and service, and anticipates the future. In order to give voice to community college students, a president has to master the skills of advocacy.

References

Association of Community College Trustees Staff (eds.). *The Trustee's Role in Effective Advocacy*. Washington, D.C.: ACCT, 2009.

Harbour, C., and Day, M. "Negotiating the Community College Institutional Environment." In C. P. Harbour and P. L. Farrell (eds.), *Contemporary Issues in Institutional Ethics* (p. 7). San Francisco: Jossey-Bass, 2009.

Kazis, R. "State Policy and Advocacy for Student Success." *Community College Journal*, April 2006, 50.

Phelan, D. J. "The Changing Role of the President as a Fiscal Leader." In *Sustaining Financial Support for Community Colleges*. New Directions for Community Colleges, no. 132. San Francisco: Jossey-Bass, 2005, 87–98.

Schreiber, Martin H., II. "UM Dean Profited While Students Faced Tuition Hikes." *Baltimore Sun*, February 3, 2010. Retrieved November 17, 2011, from http://articles .baltimoresun.com/2010-02-23/news/bal-deanletter0222b_1_questionable-payments -tuition-students.

Spilde, M. "Let Our Story Be Known." *Community College Journal*, February 2010, 6.

MARY ELLEN DUNCAN, *PhD, is a retired president of Howard Community College, Columbia, Maryland.*

CALVIN BALL, *EdD, is a professor at Morgan State University, Baltimore, Maryland, and an elected member of the Howard County Council.*

7

This chapter explores what being a leader at the community college means, what the threats are to effective leadership, and what factors leaders should be especially concerned with as colleges face new challenges and demands. Several key ideas about leadership are presented.

Leadership: A Balancing Act

Thomas E. Hines

Introduction

When I first began writing this chapter, I thought of using an analogy of a high-wire circus performer to illustrate the balancing act necessary to be an effective leader. But the more I thought about it, the more I realized that a better metaphor employs a seesaw rather than a high wire. True, a high-wire performer must understand the critical nature of balance in determining continued success. The high-wire expert's challenge may also partly describe some of the challenges a community college president experiences—that is, a certain degree of vulnerability and, in some cases, loneliness.

Nevertheless, the seesaw seems more appropriate to describe the community college environment. After all, how many times do we have activities, projects, and efforts that involve only one person? Plus, I can think of many fun comparisons that use the seesaw. What about the bully in the playground who sometimes pounces on one end of the seesaw in order to send the unsuspecting kid on the other end into the air? Returning to the metaphor as it relates to leadership, maintaining balance can be difficult because balance is affected by the personality, strengths, and attitudes of the leader as well as the complicated environment within and outside the community college itself.

NEW DIRECTIONS FOR COMMUNITY COLLEGES, no. 156, Winter 2011 © 2011 Wiley Periodicals, Inc.
Published online in Wiley Online Library (wileyonlinelibrary.com) • DOI: 10.1002/cc.468

In this chapter, we examine leadership as it relates to various environments and how we can maximize our own potential in order to maximize the potential of the colleges we serve.

Robert Fulghum (1989) subtitled one of his first books *Uncommon Thoughts on Common Things*. In this chapter, we certainly consider the usual and traditional aspects of leadership as they relate to community colleges. However, we also explore alternative, less common ideas related to leadership.

Leadership and Context

To begin, let us define what we mean by leadership. *Leadership* is the motivating force that inspires both individuals and organizations to reach their highest potential and to achieve their mission and goals. That is why leadership is so critical. Effective leadership requires positive action and results. However, if our goals are inappropriate or uninspiring, the action and results also are likely to be ineffective or deficient. If the leader is unable to relate to and inspire others, the organization is not likely to thrive and grow.

Whether we are thinking about our own personal leadership situation or about leadership from the perspective of hiring and job assignments, the context is also extremely significant. How do the leaders (and other participants) fit with the particular situation or job at hand? Like putting a square peg into a round hole, the situation and the organization's needs sometimes do not match the people we assign to do various jobs. However, often there are good reasons to ensure that a team has balance and diversity in its membership.

Consider planning, for example. There are several key components to the total process. There is the need for formal assessments that relate to the success of staff and students. Other areas that need to be assessed include the college community itself and the outside community in terms of its perceived needs and how well the college is addressing those needs. The total planning process itself should be assessed.

But assessment is only one component. Planning also involves reviewing institutional goals as they relate to needs. It involves big-picture thinking and brainstorming to enable the college to identify new directions and to deal with them creatively. Therefore, often it is appropriate to include a diverse group of people on a team. Another alternative is to involve more than one group in planning and other complicated processes.

Context is also important in terms of determining whether the leader is a good fit for the particular leadership position. While the search and selection process should help determine the candidates whose strengths best fit the college's needs, glitches sometimes result in poor hiring decisions. Ideally, the candidates themselves should help with the process through self-selection, because a leader who does not match the needs of the community college is likely to be dissatisfied as well as ineffective.

NEW DIRECTIONS FOR COMMUNITY COLLEGES • DOI: 10.1002/cc

About *You*

You may be reading this chapter and thinking about your own potential as a leader. You may be thinking about becoming a president. You may be a new college president who is preparing for your first assignment. Or you may be a seasoned leader who wants to move to the next level and serve your college more effectively.

Whatever your goals, a good place to start is with yourself. That is probably a subject that you are more familiar with than any other. Also, it is helpful to understand how you interact with other people. If you have not already completed a personality inventory, it is something you should consider. Some of these inventories are free and available online. Try Googling "free online personality inventories" to locate one. The results will provide additional insight about yourself and how you function, especially in relation to others. The Myers-Briggs inventory, for example, identifies your style as fitting into one of sixteen personality "types" (www.myersbriggs.org).

In all probability, you are not going to change your personality or behave much differently as a result of taking an inventory. However, you can identify your own style and how you tend to deal with other people. Some people's interaction styles may present you with more challenges than others. You have probably heard of the WIFM principle: "What's in it for me?" Most of us are interested in how plans and changes will affect *us*. So, why not be sure that you interact with others effectively and provide them with an understanding of what proposals and changes will mean for *them*? In order to empathize with others, we need to understand how we are perceived and how we interact. Then we can be sure that our communications focus on how the receiver of our messages will react to what we are saying.

When you think about it, usually there are several ways to send a message. Why not choose to frame your message from the perspective of your audience—that is, help them understand what is in it for them and why your ideas are important and worthy of their personal investment?

The Good, the Bad, and the Ugly

One of my favorite movies is *Hoosiers* (Anspaugh, 1986). Based on a true story, the film about a small-town Indiana basketball team winning the Indiana state championship is certainly exciting enough. However, for me, the characters and their development are what make this movie special.

In many ways, *Hoosiers* is a classic underdog story. Coach Dale's "team" started as an undisciplined group of players who thought they knew it all. The coach's first challenge was to work with them on fundamentals and discipline. During one game, his tough discipline even included playing with only four players! Dale employed Shooter, the town drunk and father of one of the players, as an assistant. But Dale did not get much help from his assistant until he helped Shooter overcome his addiction to alcohol.

Impressed with Coach Dale's integrity, Jimmy, the town's star basketball player, decided to join the team later in the year. Together, with hard work and discipline, this small team went on to win the Indiana State basketball championship. What a story!

This movie provides us with several important lessons about leadership. First, there is an important lesson about people and the fact that they can and do make dramatic positive changes in their lives. Another lesson is that people who lead must be courageous. They are not always liked and revered for their efforts. Third, hard work that often focuses on the fundamentals is essential to success. Fourth, risk is a factor that leaders should embrace. Coach Dale risked his own job by making tough decisions about how his team should function. He also took a major risk by giving Shooter the chance to succeed, even when everyone else had abandoned him. The final lesson is that small organizations, often lacking resources and having many other challenges with which to deal, can be highly successful and achieve greatness.

Think about this story in relationship to community colleges. One of the really *good* qualities of community colleges and their leaders is that they provide a wide variety of people with new possibilities. Just talk with a few community college professionals and you will hear countless stories of people who have overcome major obstacles and succeeded: Students who began their work by earning a general equivalency diploma and then went on to earn an associate degree. Senior citizens in their nineties who enroll and graduate just because they have always wanted to complete a college degree. Honors students who are also single moms or single dads. Workers who have lost their jobs and are retraining for new, technologically advanced careers. The list goes on and on.

Certainly, community colleges have strong, effective leaders. Just as Coach Dale had to work with a group of players who thought they knew it all (and had always done it that way), there are many college leaders who have to deal with similar issues. The *good* thing is that we have leaders who are courageous enough to make difficult decisions. Another real strength is that these same leaders are willing to take some risks to provide the guidance and encouragement necessary for the success of others.

What about the *bad*? you may be asking. The *bad* is also evident in community colleges, just as it is in other kinds of organizations. A more positive and proactive way to work with bad situations is to consider them opportunities. Whether these challenges are a lack of resources, bad attitudes of certain faculty and staff, a community that is not particularly supportive of the college, or political pressures from people who do not necessarily have the best interests of the college in mind, each challenge must be confronted and resolved in a positive way. The effective leader is capable of helping the college deal with problems as well as new possibilities.

NEW DIRECTIONS FOR COMMUNITY COLLEGES • DOI: 10.1002/cc

However, bad situations become *ugly* when leaders are either incapable or unwilling to do their jobs and deal effectively with problems. As an example, an employee who treats students badly and whose attitude is not in line with the mission of the college is a problem. The problem becomes ugly when there are no appropriate guidelines and processes to foster the positive learning environment that should exist. Leaders are responsible for shaping the attitudes and culture of the organization. They are also responsible for seeing that there is a fair and effective process to deal with inappropriate, negative behaviors of staff, faculty, and students. In some cases, reassignment or even dismissal may be necessary. Leaders who ignore the problem often prolong bad situations and also lose the respect of the people who work for them.

Another leadership problem that I consider to be in the ugly category is micromanagement. The reason that this problem is so critical is that it usurps the creativity and energy from otherwise talented faculty and staff. I have always believed that key leaders who are unable to delegate and let others do their jobs are either insecure or arrogant. Their behavior often results in other serious problems, such as an unwillingness of employees to take responsibility for their actions and decreased employee motivation.

Micromanagement by the community college's board can also be a major stumbling block. Assuming the president is fortunate enough to have an effective, well-functioning board, the board chair can often talk individually with one or two board members who are trying to micromanage the college or the president. Another helpful strategy is to have a board retreat that includes some discussion of appropriate board roles as well as negative, inappropriate board member behaviors. State associations as well as national associations, such as the Association of Community College Trustees, can be helpful in providing these kinds of educational sessions for boards of trustees. If the president is experiencing this kind of difficulty, it is important to deal with the concern as soon as possible before it becomes even more serious.

A final example of a serious leadership problem (ugliness) is the leader who lacks integrity. It is almost always impossible for leaders who cannot take personal responsibility and deal honestly and positively with others to be effective role models and to set a positive tone for an organization. If your credibility as a person and a leader is questionable, it is highly unlikely that people will trust you enough to follow you—in which case, your employer should probably replace you.

Fortunately, community colleges have many strong leaders. However, all of us can continue to work on building our effectiveness and improving on what we do. There are two important elements to making transformational change in ourselves and in the organizations we serve. The first element is being receptive to criticism and new possibilities. The second ingredient for change is to *begin*—do something to initiate the change process in yourself and/or others.

Moving from Good to Great

Jim Collins's book *Good to Great* (2001) is an interesting look at a few excellent companies that have risen quickly from the ranks of "good" to being judged "great" in a number of significant ways. Collins worked with an extensive research team over a period of five years to identify organizations that had suddenly moved to a higher level and outperformed the market for a subsequent period of at least fifteen years.

One of the premises of the book is that "good" is the enemy of "great." By that, Collins means that most organizations do not attain greatness because they are satisfied with good, or even very good, performance. The same is true for individuals, many of whom become good at what they do but rarely achieve greatness.

As a community college leader, I found the challenge of defining greatness almost as challenging as helping an organization achieve it.

There are some 1,200 community colleges in the United States now, and the American community college has been an innovative and productive success story since the first public community college, Joliet, was founded in Illinois more than 100 years ago. By most standards and measures of success, such as student academic measures, certification examination results, contributions to the economic and educational well-being of the communities served, and measures of value as compared to cost, most of our community colleges are performing extremely well.

However, how do we define *great*, and (more important) how do we accomplish the necessary goals to become great? Quality has to be defined in some context, and our academic accreditation processes have helped to provide this context by defining outcome levels that are considered acceptable when comparing or judging one's own organization against similar academic institutions. In addition, other benchmarks serve as useful tools for comparison purposes.

In *Good to Great*, Collins (2001) also develops a metaphor called the *hedgehog concept*—the notion that the complex world can be simplified into a single, basic principle that unifies, organizes, and guides all of our decisions. The concept comes from a comparison of a hedgehog to a fox— something like the story of the tortoise and the hare. The fox hurries to get ahead, rushes from one great idea to another, and is always interested in the next big possibility. The hedgehog, in contrast, has a constant routine that focuses on getting the job done. An example is that for protection, the hedgehog curls into a little ball and exposes its spines.

Using the hedgehog concept successfully requires that the organization clearly define how to produce the best long-term results and also refuse to pursue opportunities that do not fit with its "self-concept." Obviously, developing a workable, unifying concept for an organization may take some time. Nevertheless, leaders who have succeeded in helping their organizations simplify and focus on a unifying concept often have enabled their institutions to be judged as great.

Collins is now working on applying the same methodology used to identify great corporations to other types of institutions. Before presenting the results of these long-term studies, Collins wrote a monograph entitled *Good to Great and the Social Sectors* (2005). Part of his initial work involved critical feedback, structured interviews, and laboratory work with more than 100 social-sector leaders.

Collins has identified four basic output variables for great institutions.

1. *Performance* includes objective measures, possibly including factors such as graduation rates or test scores.
2. *Impact* involves identifying what would happen if the institution did not exist. In other words, how is the organization unique or special?
3. *Resilience* refers to the ability of an institution to survive a difficult time and to emerge stronger than before.
4. *Longevity* requires that an organization sustain all of the other variables (high performance, unique impact, and resilience) over a long period of time.

Consider what factors might make a community college unique or special; what performance factors are most important; what levels of performance are necessary to reach true excellence; and what kinds of major challenges would have to be overcome to demonstrate resilience. Educators sometimes believe that performance in educational institutions cannot be measured as effectively as it can be in other kinds of organizations. However, it is essential that institutions identify appropriate measures and require staff to rigorously collect evidence to track progress. Otherwise, how will we know how we are doing and what we need to do to improve?

If we think about American community colleges in general and what has made these organizations special over the past several decades, what unique characteristics would we consider? On my list, I would include access, innovation/agility (ability to create and to change quickly), and community focus/responsiveness as key ingredients that set community colleges apart from other institutions of higher education.

Assume that in addition to being effective teaching and learning organizations, community colleges meet several other criteria. They maintain their "open doors" and remain accessible for the diverse groups of people they serve. They continue to respond creatively and quickly to change and meet new community educational needs. They remain closely connected to the communities they serve. What factors will then separate the *good* from the *great*?

In all likelihood, the great community colleges will be those that have the highest scores on all of the criteria. If leaders of these organizations are similar to the great companies studied by Collins, they will get the right people in the right positions. Hiring the best people and dealing with poor or ineffective employees are major challenges within the college environment—especially if there are unions involved. I suggest starting with the hiring process, attracting the best possible candidates with a passion to do their best and actively developing these employees. Then leaders must develop a clear vision to enable the college to serve a unique role. They will have to decide what their particular strengths are and in what areas they will excel.

The best community colleges will be the most agile, innovative, and able to quickly design and offer high-quality instruction that meets both current and emerging demands in the marketplace. Because community colleges must meet community needs, and their missions are continually expanding, the greatest challenges may be defining and focusing on the specific areas in which they can excel and finding the resources to do it. The hedgehog concept is a difficult principle for community colleges because their missions are so diverse and community needs are so great.

The challenge of the hedgehog concept requires that leaders work with faculty and staff to focus on areas that develop the core areas of the college's mission. It means that colleges must set and work on priorities that are aligned with their missions. It also means that leaders must identify areas that are *not* central to the college's mission and do not serve to move the college toward greatness. Usually, if the leader works with staff to identify both the priorities and the resources necessary to implement the priorities, it is much easier to eliminate those activities that do not focus on the college's central mission. There are only so many resources available to meet critical needs.

According to Collins, *greatness* is not an *end point*. It is a dynamic process. Greatness is not a function of circumstance. It is largely a matter of conscious choice and discipline (2005). The challenge for the community college leader, then, is to help the college attract and develop the best staff and to develop the discipline and processes to achieve the desired results.

Future Expectations

It is certainly difficult to try to predict the future, but scanning the past and present can be a great help to presidents and other leaders who seek to plan effectively. A good understanding of the past helps professionals understand the college culture and how they arrived in their present situation. It is important to understand the present environment in order to be able to deal with and shape the future.

My colleagues in the stock brokerage business used to say that the "trend is your friend." I am sure that they were describing long-term trends. Over the decades, for example, the Dow Jones average has closed from a low of 28.48 in 1896 to a high of 14,164.53 in October 2007. Obviously, there have been some serious peaks and valleys between 1896 and now. Nevertheless, it is important to think about trends that we believe are likely to continue well into the future and what those trends may require of our leaders.

The use of technology continues to accelerate. As an example, go to your browser and type "historical increases in Internet use" and peruse several pages of results. According to Internet World Stats, Internet usage in the United States has grown from 124,000,000 people (44.1 percent of the population) in the year 2000 to 239,893,600 people (77.3 percent of the population) in 2010 (Internet World Stats, Miniwatts Marketing Group, 2000–2010). We could locate many other examples of technology growth by focusing on specific areas of technology.

Educators are obviously interested in trends that relate to pedagogical needs and methods, student values, student preparation for college, and educational devices, including computers, cell phones, combination digital devices, and other new gadgets. It is probably prudent to expect a continued increase in the availability and use of technology. Educational trends appear to be very much related to the ubiquity of technology because students use these devices to learn, research, and study—not to mention the many social uses of technology.

How do we keep up with these fast changes in technology, values, needs, preparation, economic factors, demographics, and others? As part of the planning process, community colleges need to establish some kind of system to scan the environment for changes and trends on an ongoing basis. Ideally, scanning should be done every year or two; but it is especially important to include it in the college's regular planning process, which frequently covers a five-year time frame. One effective technique is to establish a small, diverse team of people who have skills in research and "future thinking." Obviously, balance in a group assembled to do this job is particularly important because the team should work together to process and discuss the various items that are brought to the table. The group's efforts should include a methodology to consider various possibilities and discuss whether there is adequate evidence that the trend is both viable and important to the future success of the college and its constituents. Also, the job of team members is to identify various sources of information that they regularly review and evaluate. At a minimum, such a team may be used to recommend reference sources that can provide appropriate data when they are needed.

Responding to ongoing trends and anticipating future needs are just the beginning. Building understanding among staff members and helping them to bring about the required changes at the college is an additional challenge. The planning process at the college may be used as a tool to help employees understand needs and priorities.

Staff members involved in these processes should be highly respected by their peers, because it is important that the information and priorities they develop and recommend be highly credible. Diversity of points of view among the participants is also important to achieving useful results. Good representation on the planning committees helps ensure that results are balanced and representative of important future directions for the college. In addition, providing other members of the college community opportunities to review and respond to the recommendations can also help ensure widespread buy-in of the various college constituencies. Sometimes it is useful to hire an outside consultant to help the groups formulate strategies and prepare for their tasks.

While we do not have a crystal ball that accurately forecasts the future, we can use talented staff and available research to help identify important trends and anticipate needs in order to plan better and meet the future needs of our students and communities.

Conclusion: Putting It All Together

When we started this chapter, I suggested that the analogy of a seesaw might be helpful as we think about leadership. I was talking recently to a friend whose career was in elementary education. She reminded me that in addition to kids who seem to enjoy jumping off or on the seesaw to see what happens to the unsuspecting kid on the other end, there is the kid who stays in the middle and attempts to help balance the seesaw. I suspect that the president of a community college is more frequently in the balancing mode than in the unbalancing mode. However, there are many times when presidents need to shake up the balance. If you happen to take over as president of an institution that has stagnated and does not have much creative energy, you may be challenged to energize the college, for example. This challenge may call for some rather abrupt changes that get people's attention.

Lists seem to be popular in our fast-paced environments today. Indeed, they are helpful because they offer a way to review quickly and consider important ideas. So, here is my list of important leadership ideas, in which I have interspersed some one-liners for your amusement.

Twenty-Two Key Ideas About Leadership in Community Colleges

1. Hire the best employees you can get, develop them, and provide them with opportunities to learn and grow.
2. "I have an understanding with my board—I don't meet without them, and they don't meet without me" (Stewart, 1988, p. 23). Maintain good informal and formal communications with your board. Assuming you have a board chair with whom you can work well, you can usually resolve problems most effectively through the chair.

3. Do not take yourself too seriously. Although your leadership is important, you may be amazed at how quickly you will be forgotten after you have left the college. "Don't be afraid what people will think—people don't think about you half as much as you think they do" (Stewart, 1988, p. 15).

4. LISTEN! This suggestion is much broader than you may realize. Think about how important it is to recognize and interact with people, especially staff. Your showing genuine interest in them helps build a culture of trust and working together for a common cause. Take time to chat with the janitors, cafeteria staff, faculty, students, and others. You will be surprised at what you learn and how much fun it can be.

5. "It's lonely at the top—it's lonely at the bottom too, but remember, the top pays more!" says George Vaughan, a friend and noted author/consultant in higher education. Do not take the job unless you believe you can do it well and maintain balance in your own life as well as the college.

6. The key enemies of greatness in the presidency are arrogance, micromanagement, shortsightedness, poor or weak hiring decisions, low expectations, lack of commitment to the hedgehog concept and overall success of the college, and the inability or unwillingness to make tough decisions.

7. Be a good follower as well as a good leader. A good follower is a team player who not only listens to and appreciates the ideas of others but also helps to develop the overall plans and directions for the college.

8. You are the leader, and people should look to you as a role model. Be sensitive to what you are modeling and whether it will serve others and the college well.

9. Balance planning with spontaneity. I believe that Tom Peters was one of the first to use the phrase *ready, fire, aim* as a mechanism to encourage organizations to be more spontaneous. Presidents must be willing to risk and to encourage spontaneity and creativity as well as long-term planning.

10. *You and they.* As a president, there are plenty of opportunities to speak, write, and *influence* others. You can also provide influence by helping others succeed, suggesting avenues to success, providing alternatives, and being an outstanding role model.

11. Balance the old with the new. Sometimes it is tempting to become overly excited about new ideas, new staff, and new directions (the hedgehog versus the fox?). But do not forget your longer-term employees who also have some good ideas *and* a historical perspective on the college from which to draw.

12. Remember *Hoosiers.* There are heroes and underdogs in almost any game. We need heroes, but we serve many underdogs as well. We hope that many of today's underdogs will become tomorrow's heroes. Certainly our job is to help all of them be successful.

13. Teaching and learning are intertwined. Help faculty develop the balance that results in successful outcomes. Faculty members need great mentors and opportunities to improve and to share their expertise.

14. Presidents need to play too! You need a life outside the college, but you also can have fun if you infuse some lighter activities into your work. Enjoy your associations with people at the college and outside the college while you perform your presidential duties.

15. Know who your enemies are. Try to work with them, if possible, and look for creative ways to diffuse their negative effects on the college and its future. An appropriate one-liner states: "It isn't enough to love flowers, you've got to hate weeds" (Stewart, 1988, p. 76). From the perspective of the overall organization, these individuals may be *weeds* in addition to being *your* enemy!

16. You cannot be the good guy all of the time. Balance constructive criticism and tough decisions with plenty of positive reinforcement. Do not underestimate the importance of a thank-you or a compliment.

17. In colleges, power is diffused. Keep in mind that there are many sources of power besides the power of position; these include the power of inclusion, power of shared ideas, power of language, power of contacts/friendships, and power related to career and economic situation. The effective president often relies on sources of influence other than the formal power of his or her position to provide strong leadership.

18. Effective college presidents embrace a vision that is much larger than themselves. "Don't major in minor things!"

19. Never underestimate the power of commitment and enthusiasm.

20. "*Greatness* . . . is largely a matter of conscious choice, and discipline" (Collins, 2005, p. 31).

21. "My advice for new college presidents: Never tell people your troubles —half of them don't care, and the other half are sort of glad it happened to you" (submitted by Dale Parnell, during his tenure as president of the American Association for Community and Junior Colleges (AACJC); Stewart, 1988, p. 93).

22. "Walk the talk." Remember that your actions speak louder than your words.

References

Anspaugh, D. (director). *Hoosiers* [film]. MGM Studios, 1986.

Collins, J. *Good to Great.* New York: HarperCollins Publishers, Inc., 2001.

Collins, J. *Good to Great and the Social Sectors.* Monograph. Boulder, Colorado: Author, 2005.

Fulghum, R. *All I Really Need to Know I Learned in Kindergarten.* New York: Willard Books, 1989.

Internet World Stats, Usage and Population Statistics, Miniwatts Marketing Group, 2000–2010. http://www.internetworldstats.com/emarketing.htm

Stewart, B. F., with Brenneman, G. *Management by One-Liners*. Washington, D.C.: American Association of Community and Junior Colleges and National Center for Higher Education, 1988.

THOMAS E. HINES, PhD, is a retired president of Spoon River College, Canton, Illinois.

8

This chapter surveys state directors and professors in community college leadership programs, as well as the writings of key analystsof higher education, for the challenges, opportunities, and central concerns they identify in the present and future of community colleges.

Further Views from Professors, State Directors, and Analysts

Arthur M. Cohen

The foregoing chapters detailed several former presidents' views of the challenges facing community colleges. This summation continues the discussion by reporting similar information gained by extending the reactions of twenty-seven professors now teaching in community college leadership programs who responded to the question, "What issues do you emphasize in your courses and what issues most concern your students/practitioners?" It also draws on a separate survey of forty-seven state directors and on the writings of four respected analysts of a generation ago: Howard Bowen, Ed Gleazer, Clark Kerr, and John Lombardi. It is not a comprehensive survey of the literature nor a randomly drawn sample of professors but a distillation of opinion shared by people who now or in the past have considered the place of community colleges in the structure of American higher education.

Most of the issues mentioned have concerned analysts for several decades, but a few are new, and all are worthy of discussion. The challenges most frequently expressed concern the three perennials: finance, vocational education, and developmental education, plus a recent addition, outcomes assessment. Also noted were these:

- Leadership development
- Transfer and articulation
- The for-profit sector

New Directions for Community Colleges, no. 156, Winter 2011 © 2011 Wiley Periodicals, Inc.
Published online in Wiley Online Library (wileyonlinelibrary.com) • DOI: 10.1002/cc.469

- Program completion rates
- Faculty concerns
- Institutional identity
- Physical plant
- Evidence-based decision making

These topics will be examined in the remainder of this chapter.

The first conclusion of this review is that every era has had its crises, but few have been resolved. New crises arise continually and shunt aside those that recently occupied center stage, and they in turn are submerged only to reappear at a later date. In the 1950s and 1960s, community colleges expanded into every state, and questions of institutional identity were prominent. In the 1960s especially, opening campuses and staffing them with faculty and administrators who understood the comprehensive mission were foremost. The 1970s saw the rise of collective bargaining and affirmative action, each of which was hailed as a panacea by some, a mortal threat by others. In the 1980s, major sources of public support shifted from localities to state capitals; in one decade, the ratio that had been one-third each for local and state became 11 percent local and 60 percent state. And in the 1990s, limitations on funding clashed with pressures for increased enrollment, as the number of eighteen-year-olds and the proportion of high school graduates in the population expanded. All these concerns are still in place. But there is an institutional constancy, a stability that has allowed the colleges to maintain themselves, an assertion demonstrated by the fact that once opened, practically none has been forced to close or merge for lack of funding or students.

Finance

A few overriding issues, with finance heading the list, have been central concerns for practitioners and analysts throughout the history of the colleges and into the present. Colleges never have enough money to satisfy all demands: There is always an aging building that needs renovation or replacement; staff members who feel underpaid; a program that should be organized or expanded; an increased student enrollment that requires additional faculty and space. Thirty-five years ago, Howard Bowen (1977), who analyzed higher education's functions, outcomes, and support, put it succinctly when he said that colleges will raise all the money they can and spend all the money they raise. Hyperbolic perhaps for some institutions, but it is axiomatic in community colleges with their open-ended goals and commitment to serve the entire population of a district with whatever form of education they desire.

Revenue generation and cost containment are clearly the chief concerns for college presidents, who spend more time on them than on any other task. The state budget allocations not only do not match the rate of inflation; recently some states, faced with their own revenue shortfalls and needs expressed by other public agencies, have reduced the per capita appropriations to the colleges. Tuition increases have accelerated; overall, community college tuition is more than double what it was ten years ago. Out-of-pocket costs for full-time, full-year, dependent students averaged $10,200 ($7,800 for students from low-income families) after grants and loans in 2007–08 (Cohen and Brawer, 2008, p. 166) All but two of the forty-seven state directors who responded to Katsinas and Friedel's 2010 survey named state and federal per capita budget reductions as the greatest threat to institutional mission. They foresaw various categories of students being shut out, especially part-time students and those not making steady progress toward completing a program. Open access and casual attendance would be severely curtailed.

College leaders have resorted to various stratagems for increasing revenue from alternative sources. Most institutions have foundations, but their median annual income is $250,000, minuscule when compared with the $9,000-per-student expenditures. Leasing of college land and facilities and seeking grants for special purposes are other popular efforts. However, the colleges have found greater success in controlling expenditures, by reducing personnel and equipment costs, by outsourcing food and services, and by cutting low-enrollment classes. Nonetheless, all efforts are blunted by the fact that the greatest expense is staff salaries and, by any measure, productivity does not increase. Education is a labor-intensive enterprise, and instructors who gain salary increases do not teach more students. Employing low-paid, part-time faculty has been the most widely used and effective mode of cost saving. Part-timers earning from one-third to one-half the per course rate account for 63 percent of the faculty, up from 41 percent thirty years ago. These are averages, though, and the wide range between college expenditures relates to salary differentials, the percent of part-time staff, and the number of higher-cost programs.

Many years ago, John Lombardi, a long-time community college president and analyst, expressed concern about the shift away from local sources of support to dependence on tuition and state funds. In 1992 he wrote:

New directions in finance are predicated on the belief that there is a way out of the financial distress now affecting community colleges. But the new directions point inward as well as outward. It is, of course, easier to seek relief from taxpayers or students than from increased productivity, better management, and less imposing edifices. But the taxpayers have become reluctant, and increasing fees and tuition may be counterproductive. Moreover, excessive dependence on augmented funds to relieve each crisis may become a ritual of self-absolution which inhibits us from seeking other, perhaps more basic causes for our troubles. We do need more money, but we are deceiving ourselves if we believe more money by itself will be a panacea or create a distinguished institution (p. 37).

Vocational Education

Jamie Merisotis, president of the Lumina Foundation, stated recently:

> [I]n order for individual citizens to prosper and for the nation to compete in the global marketplace, Americans must significantly increase their level of postsecondary attainment. . . . The economic recovery is lagging because too few workers possess the . . . skills and knowledge that can only be developed in high-quality postsecondary programs. (2010, p. 1)

His remarks summarized what innumerable commentators have reported in books, articles, and in the popular press for many decades: Higher education bears major responsibility for the welfare of the American economy.

However, this conventional belief has been challenged by several analysts. Clark Kerr, one of the leading educators of the twentieth century, agreed that "[h]igher education . . . has always served the labor market in one way or another. . . . In fact, universities began in Europe precisely for that purpose," preparing lawyers, judges, administrators, and accountants, in a curriculum that evolved to include medicine, engineering, and teaching (1994, p. 54). But, he continued: "Employers apparently have more responsibility than is generally realized. . . . A nation may advance rapidly in productivity without a significant rise in schooling attainment of the workforce." Kerr referred to the apprenticeship systems in northern Europe and Japan as examples. Furthermore, "The United States is sending work abroad . . . to be done by less-educated workers than those displaced . . . and, thus, not because of failures in the American school system" (pp. 92–93). Formal schooling "has been subject to more blame for the slowdown in productivity than can be justified; to higher expectations for near-term future contributions to an improved economy than can be met" (p. 95). Kerr quoted Lawrence Cremin's 1990 book, *Popular Education and its Discontents*, which argued that:

> to contend that problems of international competitiveness can be solved by educational reform. . . . is not merely utopian and millennialist, it is . . . a crass effort to direct attention away from those truly responsible . . . and to lay the burden instead on the schools. (p. 96)

Kerr insisted that the notion of unemployment as related to workers' schooling was not supported by the data. He cited studies showing that the education and skills level of Americans roughly match the demands of their jobs: 34 percent of the labor force does not need more than eight years of schooling for the jobs they hold; another 36 percent of jobs require up to ten years and some additional job-focused training; and 30 percent, sixteen or more years of formal education. He further broke down the requirements:

NEW DIRECTIONS FOR COMMUNITY COLLEGES • DOI: 10.1002/cc

25 percent of jobs require basic math and the ability to follow verbal instructions; 25 percent, the additional ability to follow complex written instructions; 25 percent require specialized skills learned on the job; and 25 percent, advanced knowledge and skills. "This distribution is roughly paralleled by the actual education of the American labor force" (1994, pp. 104–105).

Lombardi too questioned whether vocational education was efficient or well guided: "Are there really so many jobs awaiting our graduates as we are told? If so, are none of the unemployed qualified to take the jobs?" Many need training that can better be provided by the employer. "When the jobs are there the people will learn to use the tools." Most large industries are automated and require only a few hours or days of training. Some skills are more readily learned in school, especially those that require formal education for licensure. "But these jobs are not in the majority. . . . Would the millions of unemployed be hired if they learned a skill?" Unemployment is only minimally related to the pool of people who know how to work (Lombardi, 1992, pp. 81–82).

Kerr's writings indicate agreement: "Management has probably more total responsibility for changes in productivity than does any other segment of American society" by, among other ills, not investing sufficiently in on-the-job training. "Guilt rests more with those who overemphasize the role of schooling in the decline of the economy" (1994, pp. 103–104). Since a major proportion of manufacturing jobs have been exported, increasing numbers of remaining jobs require generic skills and traits: basic computational and linguistic literacy, desire to work, cooperative demeanor, and tendency toward promptness and regular appearance. The so-called skills gap is, in reality, another term for *work ethic*. Kerr's comments on the absurdity of blaming the schools for the comparative decline of the American economy include the compelling statement: "Seldom in the course of policy making in the United States have such firm conclusions rested on so little convincing evidence" (p. 88).

Still, the pressure for more emphasis on vocational training in community colleges comes from several sources, not least from college leaders seeking the greater per student funding that accompanies it. It comes also from corporate executives who enjoy the greater profits that attend pools of workers trained at public expense. And college leaders know that legislators respond positively to assertions that expanding vocational programs will reduce unemployment. None dare say they need additional support so that they can help students find meaningful lives. Students attend for various reasons having nothing to do with work, say the authors of *College as a Training Ground for Jobs*: "The development of values and attitudes . . . is probably of more use to employers than specific knowledge" (Solmon, Bisconti, and Ochsner, 1977, p. 160).

At the close of 2010, nearly 15 million Americans were seeking employment; over 4.5 million of them had been unemployed for more than one year; 19 percent were four-year college graduates, and another 27 percent had an associate degree or some college experience (U.S. Department of Labor, 2010). Had all of them suddenly become unskilled and forgotten how to work? Or had their jobs been downsized, automated, or exported out from under them? Furthermore, when residential construction revives and huge numbers of the currently unemployed resume working in the building trades and in real estate, furniture, home appliance, and insurance sales, will their employers insist they have college degrees? This is not to say that college is useless but that linking it to employment in more than, say, 25 to 30 percent of the workforce is misguided.

Developmental Education

Developmental, aka remedial, education has been a feature of postsecondary education for more than a century. All community colleges devote a sizable percentage of their curriculum to it and spend, on average, 20 percent of their instructional budgets on developmental courses and programs; overall, this amounts to $1.5 billion annually (U.S. Department of Labor, May 2011). Because of their general policy of attempting to educate practically anyone who applies, they are considerably more involved with literacy development than are the institutions that exercise selective admissions.

The term *developmental education* encompasses college efforts to bring students to the level of literacy in computation and communication required for success in the program in which they are enrolled. It has been a special concern since the 1960s, when various education requirements were reduced in most secondary schools, when four years of English became three and two years of math and science became one each. Subsequently, scores for students taking American College Testing (ACT) or Scholastic Aptitude Test (SAT) exams and for those comprising the National Assessment of Educational Progress's seventeen-year-old sample population declined until the 1980s, when they stabilized. The school reforms that were supposed to restore rigor in the curriculum, widely publicized since the 1990s and the more recent No Child Left Behind efforts, have done not nearly enough to ameliorate the problem.

Several issues surround developmental education: the types of measurement and the minimum scores used in deciding course placement for entering students; whether students should be mainstreamed or segregated; best methods of teaching functional literacy; the amount of effort devoted to working with feeder high schools; and whether remedial-course credit should be counted toward graduation are but a few of the most prominent. State and federal pleas to elevate student achievement have had little effect, even though mandated testing has been installed in half the states and some have decreed that developmental education not be offered in the public universities.

NEW DIRECTIONS FOR COMMUNITY COLLEGES • DOI: 10.1002/cc

Efforts to resolve the issues are made continually. The integrated program, combining basic literacy instruction with counseling, tutoring, and study skills seminars, is a popular approach. Summer bridge programs, learning communities, reproducible instruction offered through learning laboratories, and supplemental instruction for students in high-risk courses are also widespread techniques. Colleges have arranged an ever-changing variety of approaches. Although extramural mandates have prodded them to greater effort, these attempts predate such stimuli. A major shift in college culture has occurred though, as two options have become unacceptable: allowing sizable percentages of matriculants to fail and/or drop out, and reducing academic standards so that those who do get through have not been sufficiently prepared for either subsequent studies or the workplace. More generally seen now are college efforts to drop the three Rs and English as a second language entirely from the graded curriculum.

Outcomes Assessment

Outcomes assessment is the only one of the four major issues noted that would not also have been named in past years. About twenty years ago, after decades of ineffective requests from a small group of analysts and psychometricians, the accrediting associations started pushing the colleges to define and document outcomes. Until then, researchers and commentators had made little headway in convincing educators to specify in measurable terms just what they were trying to teach and how much success they were having; the importunateness hardly penetrated the world of educational practice. But gradually the state legislatures began making demands for evidence not only of student attainment but also of college contributions to the broader community. Then the U.S. Department of Education (USED) muscled its way into the conversation, even to the point of suggesting a national collegiate assessment system, which hit the educational community like a bucket of ice water. Now outcomes assessment is a serious consideration on every campus.

Just as community colleges have many roles, assessing their contributions takes many forms. State pressures for assessment date to Florida's College-Level Academic Skills Tests, mandated in 1982. And since 1988, USED has stipulated that for accrediting agencies to be on its approved list, they must demand that colleges specify their objectives and conduct studies regularly to determine the extent to which those objectives are being met. Compliance has been slow but with prodding from the accreditors, the colleges are coming around. In addition, nearly all the states demand some form of performance accountability, sometimes tying a portion of funding to the requirement. The most common measures are rates of student graduation, transfer, licensure-exam passing, and job placement.

Another type of outcomes assessment relates to college impact on the community in two ways: enhancing human capital and direct effects.

Academic (general), vocational, and developmental education augment human capital. The first contributes to good citizenship, as highly educated people are more likely to vote, to participate in charitable organizations, and to maintain stable family lives and are less likely to be unemployed or engage in criminal behavior. Vocational education leads to employment at higher wages, hence to people paying more taxes and to practitioners providing essential services. Developmental education produces a more literate populace that can follow written instructions, ranging from electoral ballots to nutritional guidelines.

Economic impact studies that assess direct financial contributions have also been attempted. Four types of benefits are usually included:

1. College expenditures on salaries
2. Students' expenditures while they are enrolled and the higher taxes they pay subsequently
3. Reduced number of welfare recipients and prison populations
4. Overall return to the public relative to their support of the colleges

Over 500 such studies have been conducted in the past twenty years, some attributing benefits to single colleges, others linking all the colleges in a state. College chief executive officers and trustees applaud these studies because they invariably shine a favorable light on their institution: salaries paid, and the living expenses incurred by staff and students augment the local economy; graduates earn more; former students place less demand on public funds; and the money spent to support the college is always less than the presumed economic gain it engenders. These reports are often widely publicized in the local press through laudatory headlines and editorials. However, they tend to be discounted by legislators who recognize their obvious assuredly positive outcomes, and know that an audit of a prison, sanatorium, or hospital would yield similarly salutary fiscal returns.

Until the relatively recent insistence on outcomes assessment, institutional research had a low priority, often given over to untrained staff. Few colleges had more than one or two full-time equivalents in their research office, if they even had such an entity. Now, with the extramural insistence on particular forms of data, institutional researchers are kept busy turning out compliance reports. Producing data on vocational program completion and job attainment and on graduation and transfer rates is a considerable improvement over the previous laissez-faire approach to student entry and exit. Ideally, outcomes would be linked to the practices that lead to higher or lower attainment. But research in education, indeed in all the social sciences, is not sufficiently exact so that one can say with confidence that this outcome resulted from that manipulation. All searches for hyperconnectivity are futile.

The practice of hypothesizing, conducting trials using randomly selected experimental and control groups, and making decisions based on the findings is well advanced in the physical and life sciences. Although distant from even occasional practice in education, the minuscule number of such studies that have been reported show promise. One of them assigned full-time students at random to learning communities, resulting in their taking and passing more courses and showing greater gains in English proficiency than did their counterparts who were not so guided (Jaschik, 2008). In another study, randomly selected low-income parents attending the college were given $1,000 per year scholarships in addition to the financial aid for which they were qualified. That group was more likely to enroll full time, pass more courses, and return for successive semesters (Brock and Richburg-Hayes, 2006). In sum, specially designed experiences can be salutary and research can demonstrate their value.

Further Concerns

A few of the leadership program professors mentioned each of the following issues.

Leadership Development.   Leadership development has several facets, with grooming people to succeed retiring presidents high on the list. The day is long past when it was feasible to select someone from the lower administrative ranks and hand them the keys a few weeks ahead of the president's leaving. Now lengthy searches are conducted, and, for better or worse, the preferred candidates are those with experience as presidents elsewhere, even if a cloud hovered over their leaving their prior position.

A few respondents mentioned the need for revised governance and management that would reflect the complexities of the contemporary colleges. But none referred to the program planning and budgeting system, program evaluation and review technique, management by objectives, or total quality management that had been prominent in the literature formerly. What happened to them? Have they been so integrated into college management that they are no longer goals to be sought? Or have they been supplanted by the current darling, objectives-based decision making? And, if so, will that too eventually fall into the dustbin of failed ideas?

Transfer and Articulation.   Transfer and articulation has long been an issue, gaining even greater prominence recently as cost and availability have driven more highly qualified students to the community colleges. The so-called seamless system, reaching from kindergarten to graduate school, is still in the realm of fantasy, but some moves have been made to establish transfer associate degrees that are recognized by universities as qualifying entry to their junior class. The Community College Baccalaureate, now authorized in fourteen states, suggests another attempt to relieve the logjam at the end of grade 14, although to date it has been devoted almost entirely to vocational programs: nursing, teaching, and business.

For-Profit Sector.   Competition from and cooperation with the for-profit sector discomfited a few respondents. At bottom is the question of what makes the community college experience unique. Those liberal arts colleges that survived the growth of universities in the past hundred years and did so more because of their emphasis on social interaction among students and staff. Community colleges have campuses and amenities rarely seen in for-profit schools, and, although 63 percent of their faculty are part time, full-timers teach most of the courses, plan curricula, advise students, and participate in academic governance. To date, few instances either of damaging competition or of cooperation between the sectors have been reported. But more than a few community college trustees and administrators might experience a bit of secret joy each time one of the neighboring for-profits is investigated for overstating the benefits achieved by its enrollees.

Program Completion.   Attempts to increase program completion rates, an important consideration in the public perception of a college's worth, have spawned a variety of interventions: Designing pre-college experiences for new entrants, strictly enforcing deadlines for course enrollment, establishing learning communities, and encouraging faculty to reach out to students who are not attending class regularly are but a few of the numerous efforts.

Faculty Concerns.   Faculty concerns covered a wide range, including ways of selecting instructors who see themselves as enablers committed to the discipline of instruction (defined as effecting student learning) rather than as people sorters protecting the teachers of succeeding courses and eventual employers from the unskilled. Faculty productivity and the pros and cons of adjunct faculty were also considered under the unremitting question of whether the college that relies on high proportions of part-timers is sacrificing quality on the altar of saving money.

Institutional Identity.   Several decades ago, the president of the American Association of Community and Junior Colleges cautioned, "Institutions will have to be clearer about what they are and what they intend to be. . . . They cannot do everything" (Gleazer, 1973, p. 195). At that time, the issue related especially to program planning. Now it is more a question of public perceptions. If high school instructors and counselors advise their students that a college provides a clear, economical path to the baccalaureate, a large number of full-time, well-prepared students will matriculate. If a college is seen as having strong relationships with major employers, it will attract their support and students seeking skills suited particularly for those industries. If it has a reputation as an effective second-chance institution for adults who left the lower schools without diplomas, it will enroll many short-term attendees needing general equivalency diplomas. These perceptions have long-lasting, readily discernible influences on the college's transfer, job placement, and dropout rates.

Physical Plant.   Building construction and renovation was high on the state directors' list of contemporary issues, while campus safety was cited by a few of the professors. State money for construction has all but

dried up, and aging buildings get little attention unless they are in immi-
nent danger of collapsing. Similarly, although campus safety had been a
consideration since the colleges expanded the number of night classes,
security guards and major improvements in lighting were slow to arrive
until the tragedy at Virginia Tech in April 2007. Since then, campus surveil-
lance and alarm systems have gained high priority.

Evidence-Based Decision Making.   The contemporary demands for
documenting outcomes have led to calls for evidence-based decision making, a term that has become a mantra intoned by many but practiced by few.
When applied to entire programs, it requires not only linking information
about costs and outcomes, itself a challenging process, but also about the
types of staff involved and the political support that the program enjoys,
both intra- and extramurally. Decisions are considerably easier to make
when they cause the least disruption, such as changing the time that a class
meets.

Summary and Conclusions

The sources that have informed this chapter—state directors and professors
in Community College Leadership Programs and the writings of a few
selected analysts—by no means cover the breadth of opinions that might
have been revealed by a wider search. But a number of the main issues have
been brought forward. Chief among these is the bedrock principle that the
community college is a public agency and its support depends on perceptions of its value by the public (especially as represented in the legislatures)
that may relate only tangentially to its outcomes. Its main product, human
learning, is infinite, transcending college contributions to the economy and
the social justice concerns dear to many.

For most of their history, the major function of community colleges
was to serve everyone, to maintain an open door. Open access and unlim-
ited growth were heralded as public goods, and the enrollment rate was the
primary criterion of college success. This measure served the colleges well
through the third quarter of the twentieth century. In state after state, legislation was passed enabling local districts of statewide entities to organize
community colleges, with the written or tacit assumption that if college
managers could bring in students and provide staff to teach and counsel
them, the money to pay for that would be forthcoming. But in the past
thirty-five years, local fund sources have diminished, and legislatures in
many states have put limits on the number of students they will support.
The era of unrestricted growth has passed, and intense competition
between the colleges and other public agencies has become the norm.

Years ago, Howard Bowen said that higher education's main purpose
should "change from that of preparing people to fill particular slots in the
economy and of adding to the GNP [gross national product] to that of preparing them to achieve personal fulfillment and of building a civilization

compatible with the nature of human beings and the limitations of the environment" (1977, p. 459). But college leaders, aware that legislators do not accord high priority to those goals, have responded to the challenge of funding limitations by publicizing their contributions to the economy ever more vigorously.

Still, prebaccalaureate studies centering on general education and the liberal arts account for just under half the associate degree awards, a higher percentage than at any time since the 1970s, when vocational education began its forceful march. They reflect not a shift in philosophy but a reaction to the higher tuition of universities and their impacted freshman classes that have driven greater numbers of baccalaureate-bound students to community colleges.

Developmental education runs a distant third to vocational and transfer education among the major functions of community colleges, but it and the vocational education gained more attention than transfer. None of the respondents expressed concern for prebaccalaureate studies. Numerous commissions and task forces that are seeking ways of easing the transition from community colleges to universities deplore the upper-division enrollment caps and agree that guaranteed credit for course completion should be the rule. But the leadership program professors and state directors seem of the same mind as the president we once asked about his college's efforts in teaching general education and the liberal arts: "Oh, that's the faculty's responsibility." Nonetheless, developmental education as an institutional priority ranks above only noncredit community education. And it is being squeezed as greater numbers of students with higher academic preparation seek courses that accommodate their desires for associate degrees and transfer.

In 2010, the percentage of unemployed four-year college graduates was half that of people with no more than high school diplomas (U.S. Department of Labor, December 8, 2010). But hardly any commentators acknowledged the correlation-equals-causation fallacy—the probability that people with reasonably well developed computation and communication skills and who are motivated by a work ethic might be quite well represented among those who enroll in higher education, that their collegiate experiences alone have little to do with their employability. Furthermore, employers' demands for degrees relate in large measure to the number of degree holders available. Community colleges would be notably affected if supermarkets and big-box stores began requiring associate degrees for their clerks and salespeople. In sum, degrees do not create jobs; job requirements stimulate degree attainment. A few decades ago, an associate degree was sufficient qualification for entry into the nursing profession. And not many years before that, it would have allowed access to a job as a school teacher.

The vocational education proportion of the overall degree production of the community colleges grew rapidly in the 1970s, reaching a high point of 72 percent of associate degrees awarded in 1985. It then began declining, as the number of eighteen-year-old bachelor's degree seekers entering the colleges increased, and bottomed out at 54 percent in 2004, where it has remained (Cohen and Brawer, 2008, p. 259). Nearly all the recent growth in number of degrees awarded has been in arts and sciences or general programs.

Vocational education's future is unclear, clouded for now by claims that it should be focused on reducing unemployment; but it is not well positioned for that task. For the past two decades, the U.S. employment market has been experiencing a distinct shift. Job availability has expanded in both high-skill, high-wage occupations and in low-skill, low-wage jobs, while the proportion of middle-skill, white-collar clerical and sales jobs has contracted, along with blue-collar production, craft, and operative functions. This has happened because of automation and the offshoring of the types of routine tasks that were performed formerly by workers with high school or some college experience but usually less than four-year degrees. These midlevel workers—those served by the community colleges—suffered the greatest loss of employment in the recession that began in 2008. The data do show that people with higher levels of education earn more and are less likely to be unemployed. But structural unemployment is a prominent phenomenon now, as technology and globalization have enabled U.S. companies to produce and sell more without employing more workers in the United States.

The U.S. Department of Labor (May 4, 2011) has predicted that by 2018, 37 percent of new jobs will be held by people with no more than a high school education; 30 percent by those with associate degrees or some college, or no degree; and 33 percent by holders of bachelor's or higher degrees. Two or more decades ago Kerr (1995) and Lombardi (1992) predicted these proportions. The greatest number of job openings between 2008 and 2018 will be home health care aides and personal and home care aides—that is, those at the bottom of the education hierarchy. The greatest percentage of job growth will be in those requiring bachelor's or graduate degrees: biomedical engineers, network systems and data communications analysts, financial examiners, and medical scientists. The highest number of openings for those typically prepared in community colleges include: physician assistants, physical therapist assistants, and dental assistants (U.S. Department of Labor, 2010). Community colleges also have programs in the health aide categories, along with many other occupations that the Bureau of Labor Statistics (BLS) suggests will be filled by people gaining "short-term on-the-job training." A large unknown, then, in interpreting the BLS projections is: How many of those jobs will be taken by people with community college experience in addition to on-the-job training? The numerous assertions that a college education will be necessary for most jobs would be accurate only if the terms *well-paying* or *prestigious* were added. The account by the Lumina Foundation maintaining that "63 percent of all jobs will require postsecondary training" (Merisotis, 2010, p. 1) should have included those words.

The concerns that were most troublesome in 2010 were little different from those noted thirty or forty years earlier. Finances are in perennial short supply in institutions where costs of labor rise inexorably. Successes in developmental education have proved elusive as most of the students who failed to learn reading, writing, and arithmetic when they were young have no less difficulty after they mature. Occupational programs are safe as long as funding agencies continue looking through rearview mirrors at the jobs that were available many years ago while ignoring the increasing number of positions filled through on-the-job training and those requiring bachelor's or graduate degrees. But the community college leaders with vision would take note of the hollowed-out middle of the employment market and adjust their offering accordingly by moving along two fronts: supporting only those courses of study for which employment opportunities in the local market are available; and creating generic vocational degree programs centering on entrepreneurship, small-business management, marketing, and sustainability and conservation of resources.

References

Bowen, H. R. *Investment in Learning: The Individual and Social Value of Higher Education.* San Francisco: Jossey-Bass, 1977.

Brock, T., and Richburg-Hayes, L. *Paying for Persistence: Early Results of a Louisiana Scholarship Program for Low-Income Parents Attending Community College.* New York: MDRC, 2006.

Cohen, A. M., and Brawer, F. B. *The American Community Colleges* (5th ed.). San Francisco: Jossey-Bass, 2008.

Gleazer, E. J., Jr. *Project Focus: A Forecast Study of Community Colleges.* New York: McGraw-Hill, 1973.

Jaschik, S. "Promising Path on Remediation," *Inside Higher Education,* 2008, March 11, n.p.

Katsinas, S. G., and Friedel, J. N. *Uncertain Recovery: Access and Funding Issues in Public Higher Education.* Tuscaloosa, AL: Education Policy Center, University of Alabama, 2010.

Kerr, C. *Troubled Times for American Higher Education: The 1990s and Beyond.* Albany: State University of New York Press, 1994.

Lombardi, J. *Perspectives on the American Community College.* Washington, D.C.: American Association of Community and Junior Colleges and American Council on Education, 1992.

Merisotis, J. P. "President's Message." *Lumina Foundation Focus,* Fall 2010, 1.

Solmon, L. C., Bisconti, A. S., and Ochsner, N. L. *College as a Training Ground for Jobs.* New York: Praeger, 1977.

United States Department of Labor. Bureau of Labor Statistics, December 8, 2010.

United States Department of Labor, Bureau of Labor Statistics: *Education Pays,* May 4, 2011.

ARTHUR M. COHEN *is professor emeritus in the Department of Education at the University of California, Los Angeles.*

INDEX

Statement of Ownership

Statement of Ownership, Management, and Circulation (required by 39 U.S.C. 3685), filed on OCTOBER 1, 2011 for NEW DIRECTIONS FOR COMMUNITY COLLEGES (Publication No. 0194-3081), published Quarterly for an annual subscription price of $89 at Wiley Subscription Services, Inc., at Jossey-Bass, One Montgomery St., Suite 1200, San Francisco, CA 94104-4594.

The names and complete mailing addresses of the Publisher, Editor, and Managing Editor are: Publisher, Wiley Subscription Services, Inc., A Wiley Company at San Francisco, One Montgomery St., Suite 1200, San Francisco, CA 94104-4594; Editor, Arthur M. Cohen, Eric Clearinghouse for Community Colleges, 3051 Moore Hall, Box 951521, Los Angeles, CA 90095; Managing Editor, Gabriel Jones, c/o UCLA Graduate School of Education, 2128 Moore Hall, Box 951521, Los Angeles, CA 90095-1521. Contact Person: Joe Schuman; Telephone: 415-782-3232.

NEW DIRECTIONS FOR COMMUNITY COLLEGES is a publication owned by Wiley Subscription Services, Inc., 111 River St., Hoboken, NJ 07030. The known bondholders, mortgagees, and other security holders owning or holding 1% or more of total amount of bonds, mortgages, or other securities are(see list).

	Average No. Copies Each Issue During Preceding 12 Months	No. Copies Of Single Issue Published Nearest To Filing Date (Summer 2011)
15a. Total number of copies (net press run)	1,042	966
15b. Legitimate paid and/or requested distribution (by mail and outside mail)		
15b(1). Individual paid/requested mail subscriptions stated on PS form 3541 (include direct written request from recipient, telemarketing, and Internet requests from recipient, paid subscriptions including nominal rate subscriptions, advertiser's proof copies, and exchange copies)	538	499
15b(2). Copies requested by employers for distribution to employees by name or position, stated on PS form 3541	0	0
15b(3). Sales through dealers and carriers, street vendors, counter sales, and other paid or requested distribution outside USPS	0	0
15b(4). Requested copies distributed by other mail classes through USPS	0	0
15c. Total paid and/or requested circulation (sum of 15b(1), (2), (3), and (4))	538	499
15d. Nonrequested distribution (by mail and outside mail)		
15d(1). Outside county nonrequested copies stated on PS form 3541	127	127
15d(2). In-county nonrequested copies stated on PS form 3541	0	0
15d(3). Nonrequested copies distributed through the USPS by other classes of mail	0	0
15d(4). Nonrequested copies distributed outside the mail	0	0
15e. Total nonrequested distribution (sum of 15d(1), (2), (3), and (4))	127	127
15f. Total distribution (sum of 15c and 15e)	665	626
15g. Copies not distributed	377	340
15h. Total (sum of 15f and 15g)	1,042	966
15i. Percent paid and/or requested circulation (15c divided by 15f times 100)	80.2%	79.7%

I certify that all information furnished on this form is true and complete. I understand that anyone who furnishes false or misleading information on this form or who omits material or information requested on this form may be subject to criminal sanctions (including fines and imprisonment) and/or civil sanctions (including civil penalties).

Statement of Ownership will be printed in the Winter 2011 issue of this publication.

(signed) Susan E. Lewis, VP & Publisher-Periodicals

NEW DIRECTIONS FOR COMMUNITY COLLEGE

ORDER FORM SUBSCRIPTION AND SINGLE ISSUES

DISCOUNTED BACK ISSUES:

Use this form to receive 20% off all back issues of *New Directions for Community College.*
All single issues priced at **$23.20** (normally $29.00)

TITLE   ISSUE NO.   ISBN

_____   _____   _____

_____   _____   _____

_____   _____   _____

*Call 888-378-2537 or see mailing instructions below. When calling, mention the promotional code JBNND
to receive your discount. For a complete list of issues, please visit www.josseybass.com/go/ndcc*

SUBSCRIPTIONS: (1 YEAR, 4 ISSUES)

☐ New Order   ☐ Renewal

U.S.	☐ Individual: $89	☐ Institutional: $275
CANADA/MEXICO	☐ Individual: $89	☐ Institutional: $315
ALL OTHERS	☐ Individual: $113	☐ Institutional: $349

*Call 888-378-2537 or see mailing and pricing instructions below.
Online subscriptions are available at www.onlinelibrary.wiley.com*

ORDER TOTALS:

Issue / Subscription Amount: $ _____

Shipping Amount: $ _____
(for single issues only – subscription prices include shipping)

Total Amount: $ _____

SHIPPING CHARGES:

First Item $6.00
Each Add'l Item $2.00

*(No sales tax for U.S. subscriptions. Canadian residents, add GST for subscription orders. Individual rate subscriptions must
be paid by personal check or credit card. Individual rate subscriptions may not be resold as library copies.)*

BILLING & SHIPPING INFORMATION:

☐ **PAYMENT ENCLOSED:** *(U.S. check or money order only. All payments must be in U.S. dollars.)*

☐ **CREDIT CARD:** ☐ VISA ☐ MC ☐ AMEX

Card number _____ Exp. Date _____

Card Holder Name _____ Card Issue # _____

Signature _____ Day Phone _____

☐ **BILL ME:** *(U.S. institutional orders only. Purchase order required.)*

Purchase order # _____
           Federal Tax ID 13559302 • GST 89102-8052

Name _____

Address _____

Phone _____ E-mail _____

Copy or detach page and send to: **John Wiley & Sons, One Montgomery Street, Suite 1200,
San Francisco, CA 94104-4594**

Order Form can also be faxed to: **888-481-2665**

PROMO JBNND